Sharing Spaces
Poems of the Heart

Gemma Stemley

Sharing Spaces: Poems of the Heart
Copyright © 2024 Gemma G. Stemley. All Rights Reserved.

No part of this publication may be reproduced, distributed, or transmitted in any form or by any means, including photocopying, recording, or other electronic or mechanical methods, without the prior written permission of the author, except in the case of brief quotations embodied in critical reviews and certain other noncommercial uses permitted by copyright law.

For information about this title or to order other books and/or electronic media, contact the publisher:

Gemma G. Stemley
email: gemmastemley114@gmail.com

ISBN
979-8-9919140-9-3 (Paperback)
979-8-9919140-8-6 (Ebook)

Printed in the United States of America

Cover and Interior design: Dan & Darlene Swanson
of Van-garde Imagery, Inc. • van-garde.com

For family and friends who have nurtured and sustained me.

Contents

Trinidadian Words and Phrases ix

Preface 1

1. Laudation

In Rhythm 6

The Artist 7

Mother Ma 8

My Dad 10

Ode to Mia 12

Soul Harvester 14

Mother-in-law 17

The Void, an Elegy 18

Gen Z 20

Baby Girl 22

The Death of my Student 24

Poet Laureate 26

To Billy Strayhorn 28

Young Frederick Douglass 30

Nightingale 34

2. **Landscape**

   Taxi Ride to the Beach 36

   Tropical Storm 38

   Market Scene. 40

   Song 42

   Island of Color 44

   I Know Why the Kiskadee Sings 46

   My First Snow 49

   Fall Leaves 51

   Caged Bird 53

   EL Dorado Village 55

   Paramin 57

   The Poui Tree. 59

   Full Moon 61

   Leatherback 63

   Sea Bathing. 65

   Sundrops 67

3. **Mindscape**

   Eutierria 70

   The Immigrant's Fear 72

   Exemplar 74

   Proustian 76

   First 78

   Opera 79

   On Imagination 82

Assisted Living 84

To a Genius 87

Bebop 88

The Road Well-Traveled 90

Cancer Ward 92

Double Standard 94

Leaving Home 97

The Silent 99

On Returning 100

Dawn. 102

4. **CultureScape**

Natural Healing 104

Bush Tea 106

Christmas Fare 108

Parang Party 110

Femicide 112

Mangled 113

The Plight of Bucco Reef 114

The Trinidadian Creole 115

Mamaguism 116

The Patois 118

Steelpan 122

Shango Church 124

The Priest 126

Making Callaloo 127

The Homing Instinct 129

The Chive Planters of Paramin 131

5. The Historic Landscape

Ole Time Days 134

Past Connections 138

Arrival Day in Trinidad 1845 139

Land of Sugar 140

Trailblazer 141

Indigenous 144

The Merikins of Moruga 148

Idlewild, Michigan 153

Mackinaw Island 155

History 159

The Wretched of this Earth 161

Covid 19 162

Three Fifths 164

The Weeping Time 166

At Kent State, May 4th 1970 170

Roe v Wade 171

Monticello 172

Sandy Hook and Others 175

Sundown Town 177

Trinidadian Words and Phrases

I wish to acknowledge that Rhonda S. Baptiste's useful book Trini Talk was a great help in defining some common Trinidadian words and phrases.

Aye Yai Yai-	A form of exclamation to express difficulty.
Backra Johnny	Derogatory term for a white person who supervised workers on the plantation during and after slavery.
Boo Boo man	An evil or mischievous spirit to scare children from being disobedient.
Catch your Nen Nen	Experiencing hardship.
Chantwell	A singer with a sweet voice.
Chikee-Chong	A paper kite with a long thin tail equipped with a razor blade or Zwill to destroy an opponent's kite.
Choolha	Fireside usually made from mud.
Cockset	A brand of mosquito coil used to ward of insects.

Cocoyea	The veins from coconut leaves used to make brooms also useful as a trap for song birds.
Cosquelle	Overdressed and ostentatious.
Couverte Pocham	A type of chamber pot with a lid meant to use at night before the advent of flushing toilets.
Cut-ass	Punishment in the form of a good thrashing where it hurts.
De	The
Foreday	Very early in the morning.
Grand charge	Making a big issue about nothing.
Gimme gimme	Always looking for a free handout be it money or favor.
Hold strain!	Slow down!
Jukking board	A wooden scrub board used for washing clothes.
Kow tow	To bow down in an ingratiating manner.
Lagee	A glue-like sap from the Breadfruit tree used to trap birds.
Massa Day	During the time of slavery.
No wayrian	A person who is unsure of his birthplace.
Ole	Old

One day, one day congotay	One day soon the day of reckoning will arrive.
Santimanitay	Without mercy.
Sapat	A slipper with a wooden sole and a foot band made from car tires. It looks like the modern-day Nike Slide.
Scruntin'	Experiencing hard times.
Wata more than flour	A time of great hardship
Yuh	you

Preface

Sharing Spaces: Poems of the Heart is a collection reflecting my world as an immigrant from a country, Trinidad and Tobago, I call home, to another, the United States, I have come to also accept as home. My travels often take me to lands where I am not a citizen, nevertheless, I relish opportunities to become absorbed and integrated into the landscape, culture and history of new places.

When I left Trinidad to take up studies in the US, it was for the purpose of broadening my perspective. I could have gone to Jamaica to complete my degree in Library Science but I chose to study in America. Never did I foresee problems with adjustment. The official language in Trinidad is English, but my tone and emphasis on words sometimes called into question the meaning of what I was saying. Often, I was told to slow down my pace of delivery.

As I took up studies in a rural town in Western Pennsylvania, the isolation and nostalgia I experienced were enormous, primarily brought on by a lack of access to a community of people of color, Pittsburgh being 90 miles away. Writing became my reprieve. It provided an outlet to brood over the absence of my home, a place from which I could not be turned away. At the same time, I needed to examine some aspects of acculturation while growing up under British rule which were hollow and debilitating. Separation from home and surroundings opened up access to the recesses of my mind that harbored those thoughts. I was able to explore the process in my book *Finding Home: A Sentimental Journey*.

In my world, as an immigrant, change is a constant-the landscape, relationships, past and present, the cultural milieu and the patois. I struggle with these ever-shifting currents of change. At this stage in my life, I have accepted the illusion of permanence in one place and the interplay between stability and upheaval. I live with the immigrant's fear of the call to return due to family illness or death. I experienced this last November with the passing of my brother-in-law. I am constantly living a life, ill at ease, anxious, apprehensive because I have family back home.

This relentless nature of change impels me towards new horizons turning moments of impermanence into opportunities for growth. It is the impetus for this collection of verse. I begin with Laudation which pays tribute to family and friends, some of whom are still alive while others have passed on. In subtle ways, I have been influenced by their guidance, solace and inspiration as I navigate these currents sweeping through my life.

Landscape presents the greatest challenge. Whenever I return to Trinidad, I am lost were it not for the street signs. I no longer have a circle of friends with whom I grew up, some have migrated to various parts of the world or have died. The patois changes with each passing year to the extent that I struggle to understand the meaning of words. The poems in this category are reflective, somewhat nostalgic and a bid to fence in the past.

Mindscape endeavors to harness the forces of change towards a better understanding of my world- past and present, turning moments of uncertainty into transformation. Each poem is an encounter, a beacon which it is hoped will bring clarity to the many aspects of relocation.

The group of poems under CultureScape is the oldest within the collection. Many were written during the early years of coming to America. They were attempts to find solace at a time when I was most beset by loneliness.

Poems arranged under The Historic Landscape reflect my interest in travel and history. One of my favorite exploits in locating markers on the Underground Railroad has taken me to many states in order to follow the network of freedom here in America. Together with my interest in the Orbis Spike, which attests to the deleterious effects on world climate and indigenous populations, I have become a strong advocate for revision of history. The impact of Western colonization in opening up the veins of resources flowing from countries that are today referred to as The Third World calls for re-examination. Furthermore, the adverse effects of cash crop cultivation stemming from the triangular trade of the Middle Passage have a new face-Big Farmer and its subsequent displacement of rural populations into crowded cities and ultimately the slow drift towards the boarders of developed countries in Europe and America.

Finally, I believe that the work of the poet is to explore meaning and provide insight into the human condition while at the same time sharing those spaces which connect universally.

1
Laudation

In Rhythm
(for my husband, Calvin M. Stemley)

I would be undone
ill-defined and shapeless
a melody without counterpoint, no chords
always searching for resolution
in a polyphonous song.

I would be incomplete
a quiescent pupa,
forever domed to be a chrysalis
constantly pursuing wholeness
but barred from entering its portal.

The days would slide in and out of sameness
monotonous in its drone,
no variation to contrast
no harmony-
contrapuntal and sweet.

The many elements of you in euphony
deliver me daily
wrap me into a song
with an eight-bar intro
hooking me to the verse
that touches my sweet spot
to bridge me to the chorus
where I ascend the staff
onto the octave ladder
towards vitality with you,
Virtuoso.

The Artist
(For Jannet Ruby, my sister)

Your eyes see the complexity of nature
the spider in her aerial realm
the humming bird's iridescence
the hibiscus showy style
to salute the pollinators.

You see the moment when the bursting pod explodes
to disperse her seeds
in a ballistic flight to the air.
Your eyes travel with the eagle's swoop
to snatch its prey.

You marvel at the peacock's splendor.
You hear the sound of dancer bees in the hive
in their waggle to signal the location to forage.
You capture the swagger of the elephant on canvas
and the throes of death by the hands of poachers.

You smell the earth after a down-pour
with your inner eye, you see its flow
into the underground rivers.
You comb the river banks
for the perfect granite in Venetian gold or white
to paint a quiet scene of a lighthouse.

For you are an Artist.

Mother Ma
To my Ma

You left us too soon
in your sweet quiet way
without complaint
Mother
yet you are with me.

Ma
I experience you every day.
Your light touch on my forehead
your kiss on my cheek.
Your exalting way of shouting
Bravo!
So jubilant.

Mother
I still hear your admonitions
even in my sleep
"Watch your mouth girl!"
"Don't you dare!"
"Nice girls don't"
"Yes Mom."
"Ok Mom."
"I hear you, Mom."

Ma
I often live by the precepts
you taught me
because you were wise.
You never promised me
a life free of trials

but you showed me how to brave the storms
by your example.
Mother, Ma, Mom,
I miss you.

My Dad

The only Jack of all trades and master of some
I know of.
Every day he set his path to labor,
come rain or shine, hard work,
not expecting any *gimme gimme for nothing*.
His free and easy slant to toil was rare,
I did not inherit it from him.

Never one to back-pedal on a promise
Never one to beat his own drum
Never one to *grand charge*
Never one to *kow tow* to the gentry
Never in a hurry
His mantra, "hold strain!"

I liked the way he whistled a tune
while he pottered around the house and tinker
with his old Ford
I can't remember ever hearing his singing voice,
no *chantwell* was he.

In those days when *wata more than flour*
hops bread with a dab of yellow salt butter
and a cup of Bush tea
was all
that satisfied him.

He said, "*doh hang your hat higher than you can reach.*"
But I, restless pushy ambitious
took that to be apathy,

hating the *same ole, same ole,* every day,
sought escape
a door
to the outside world
to better *meh self.*
We did not see eye to eye, always.

But maybe he feared for my safety.
He would have given his eye teeth, both
to shelter me from harm's way
he, a born-Trini-never-left
mistrustful of the outside world
and me, his forever baby girl, firstborn.
Sometimes, he would flit and flutter
to shield me.

On that fateful night
he went gentle,
a gentle man
no longer willing to put up the good fight.
I did not weep at the grave
for he is everywhere
in the tropical breeze
the rising sun
the moonbeams
on the wings of the dove.

He lives!

Ode to Mia

Sister, young enough to be progeny,
I witnessed your birth, your sprouting
like crocuses among weeds.
                You bloom.

You tower above us with your gifts.
When did you learn to walk on stilts?
My eyes are fixed to the clouds
trying to catch a glimpse of you
through the mist.
                You soar.

The overhanging dark clouds of strife
you smother.
You have no room for spite
it mars the early peeping sunrise
you lean on for vitality
                to glow.

Craft, your hands lovingly shape
into frames, that vamp the mundane,
gracing rawness with your touch,
you shape a diamond out of the rough.
                You inspire.

You are no dupe,
numbers and words,
you wade through daily,
the fine print, clothed in mystery
you tease out with ease.
                You too cool!

Your love is roomy, generous, full.
I saw how you held that urn to your chest
when you collected his ashes.
It spoke to me of volume
        You are legion.

Roses have not always been strewn along your path.
Adversity colors the human condition
but you are a master builder
you are adept at climbing those ladders
out of affliction,
        You rise!

Soul Harvester
To Dr. Richard Clarke, 9/23/1961-11/26/23

A long distant call from my nephew.
"Auntie Gemma, you need to come home!"

I can't say anything profound about death
this shifting in reality
towards a universe of sorrow
in which the question is intrinsically linked to its answer.

Some things I know and can speak with confidence-
on the wondrous symphony of life,
nature, love, music.
But of the lash of death
the clutch of dying
I am stumped.
Robbed of reason.
I am a spent force in its rendering.

The preacher declared that-
it's a deep mystery
that dying begins at the moment of birth,
that somewhere along the unfolding
life begins to lose step-
to falter here and there.
Then death takes the lead
and wins the fight
finally, to rest in the expanse
where joy and sorrow unite.

Brother-in-law

I now tread in spaces where you once habited.
I see you in memory's gaze
doing the usual things.
Never once did I think you would stride into that world-
still and silent, out of reach.

You are everywhere unceasing
in the physical.
The accoutrements of your life
linger beyond the passing
in my memory.
For instance, I look at your shoes,
with wear, worn into comfortable lines
that speak to me of assurance, no non-sense
striding in confidence.

I step into the room you most revered
Cave-like in aspect
from ceiling to floor, booked lined
that bore out your insatiable thirst for knowledge
a path to light and lore.
I did not think of a lost fight
standing in the need of prayer.

From time to time your voice floats through
singing the lyrics of a melody, in tune
of a favorite song.
As the days go by
your lost gives way to anger
not with the Maker, but with the man.
Were there not ways to forestall the advance
to hold the harvester at bay

his grim countenance to conceal?

You were the font of knowledge.
I leaned on your understanding
of the obscure-
Carl Jung, String theory, the Multiverse.
I sought you out on the nature of God,
but, strangely never on death.
It was the only rite
for which you did not expound.
Since no one has the answer.

Mother-in-law
(dedicated to Camille Stemley)

    The queen fights a protracted battle
            each day with the resolve of Job.

    Her prayer is that she can do all things
            in the Christ who strengthens her.

    Pain and discomfort she wears
            like a garment that is difficult to discard.

    The trials of life's journey have left indelible scars
            that surface to torment her

    like the demise of a child.

    The queen is no longer young,
            her body frail and delicate.

    Yet her mind is lucid
            holding onto computation and events of the past.

    She is historian, poet, educator, mathematician,
            literary expert, nurse, geologist and chef.

    The queen is now the matriarch,
            who struggles with the will to survive
                  just another day.

The Void, an Elegy
Dedicated to Zackery T. Stemley Jr.

A wintry day of drifting snow
carpeted the ground
where we stood, to say farewell.
Silently we mourned your passing at the grave-
a grim portal, indifferent to grief,
a bleak, one-way doorway
out of tribulation
to the abode of angels.

While the Old Glory shrouds your casket
your soul soars to *Taps*-
America's Song of Remembrance
rendered by the bugler,
to a true patriot.

The thirteen folds of the flag
into the triangular shape of the Trinity
attest to your faith.
Dad, was it yesterday
we talked about good times
when life was free of pain?

No longer will we hear your quiet voice
offering us counsel.
Your wisdom often shuffled the ground we tread
to bring us to the path of truth and faith,
of duty and obligation.

What of this tribute to bear of your memory,
to celebrate your life?
In this way we hope to find closure
but more so to reflect on
your final hope for us
that we may learn to vanquish
all worldly snares
in life's turbulent seas
that one day we too will
meet the Maker in glory.

Now the reality of death,
abrupt and complete, sans mercy
has seized your essence.
The sound of your voice is so soft
barely penetrating the void
you once filled.
But in memory you survive,
to flourish
for mortality is not always final.

Gen Z
(For Dr. Johnathan Clarke)

My nephew is still a Pikachu fan.
Once when he visited me
he carried his bloated mouse Pokémon
for twenty-three thousand miles by air
from Trinidad to Pittsburgh.
Then he was four.

At thirteen, running on high-speed dopamine
with the latest generation of cell phone
wedded to his headphones
he hugs his laptop
as he hustles through the airport on another visit.

At eighteen, he was no longer reachable
by snail mail or e-mail.
A text message once in a while,
perhaps through Messenger
when he was online.
Conversing without so much as a spoken word
a monosyllable or two,
never in a complete sentence.
BRB, NP, lol.

To every question-
a response of-Ok.
"How are you?" in my typical Baby Boomer-way
"Ok."
"How is school?"
"Ok."

I used to get a weekly report by phone
of activities and things.
Now I am on Face Book
just to keep up with trends.
Failing this-
I would be lost to his world.

Inept and technologically challenged
I once faced Messenger
and Skype with trepidation.
Now my laptop defrags
every two weeks on schedule.

Straddling the Gen Z wave
I am now in the 21st century.
Check out my website
http:www.wix.com/pinktulip/thereadingroom.com
my blog is still under construction,
so, be sure to look out for it.

Baby Girl
(for Dani)

I bought a little frilly dress
in pink and polka dot
with cute matching shoes
when she was four.

I filled her Christmas stockings
with toys and dolls
board games and books
to nourish her mind.

At thirteen, her taste bordered on the retro
with converse and bell bottoms.
No spaghetti straps
she selects with dad's censure in mind.

My niece is slim and graceful
in tennis skirt and Ts.
She serves with a backhand stroke
as strong as Serena's.
"Looking good kid, keep it up!"

At sixteen
she is anxious about success.
"Just do your best girl,
you don't always have to be a straight A student
none of us were."

I enjoyed it when she played the steel pan
with that melodious rhythm
with a confident hand
as fluid as cane juice.

Now she wears confidence
like a well-fitted pair of jeans.
Her thin and willowy stature
stunning, as she radiates the assurance
of the women of the Nile.

The Death of my Student

He lay regal in his coffin
the young man with a dream
to trample adversity.
Once a tower of strength
Herculean-like
He met those hard knocks, face on.

Surmounting all odds
overcoming the urge to hit rock bottom
like so many of his generation
narcotized, crushed and unstrung,
no longer will he speak the language of the masses
or be a father and son.

Cut down and thwarted
he will not see the land of his forefathers
or retrace history through the middle passage.
He will not wear the mortarboard
or graduation stole to receive his diploma
on Commencement Day
as his mother waits in the wings.

He lay in repose
without signs of the violence
that brought him down inadvertently
being in the wrong place at the wrong time.
Five or six bullets to his chest and lower abdomen.
The undertakers were skillful.

No emotion disfigured his face
no surprised look of sudden attack
disappointment and pain.
He wore a smile.

I signed the book of condolence
along with his youthful friends.
High school and college acquaintances,
his best friend and girlfriend,
class mates who flew in
the ones who drove 500 miles to say adieu
and I, who struggled to understand
this death that diminished me.

Poet Laureate

To the memory of Anson Gonzales
from Trinidad and Tobago

>The poet laureate is at the crossroads
>where images of El Viejo confront him daily.
>He has lived for so long
>he can taste his senescence.
>He sees himself disintegrating
>into the landscape of ashes
>peeling off, layer by layer
>a chip here,
>a flake there.

>The ritual of his loins
>in its nocturnal pursuit of youth
>fizzled with the passage of time.
>In its place a sigh of anguish.
>He has relinquished his harem
>long ago to the young bucks.

>Now he finds comfort only in the arms of dreams.
>He dons the aspect of old age
>wearing the raiment of patience.
>It becomes him well
>as he gives in to mortality
>waiting out time.

>He struggles to recapture the once fertile space
>where he delighted in the easy flow of words.
>The poet laureate is distressed about the truancy of his muse.
>He is anxious to be in print one last time

before his demise.

Then he remembers there once was a girl
with a heart of gold
who years ago, sent him a photograph
inscribed "with love always."
It touched his heart.
The recollection stirs him into action.

To subjugate the province of lethargy
he will get back into pumping irons.
Maybe to avert flaccidity
to regain his force.
Maybe to catch that fleeting glance.

He longs to travel the world of words again with its colors
blending them together into recondite meanings
that few can grasp,
to weft and weave a turn of phrase
into a fine tapestry
before he wears the shroud.

To Billy Strayhorn

At the age of four, Billy
you were not expected to live.
A boy growing up in poverty,
without a name
still, you were gifted.
Your music baffled the experts.
Your labor boundless-
abundant-driven
punctuating the taste of enthusiasts.

"Strays" and "Swee' Pea" friends called you,
like Nina you hoped to enter that alien world
of Classical music
but you underestimated the power of bequest.
Always out of view
cast in shadow of the sun-
The Duke,
where you thrived
to dream of a *Lush Life*
and *Something to Live For*

Your fingers like the jeweler
polished those harmonies
to a brilliant shine.
But the quality of genius is unsparing
inconsiderate.
It cares not for its holder,
its hunger ravenous

is never satisfied
until it consumes you
finally
in *Blood Count.*

Lush Life written by Billy Strayhorn between 1933-1936 released in 1948.
Something to Live For written by Billy Strayhorn in 1939.
Blood Count written by Billy Strayhorn in 1967 just before he died.

Young Frederick Douglass
(To Dr. Brian Roberts)

He heard two bells toll in harmony-
the church knell, a call to worship
and the auction bell announcing a sale
of men women and children
whom it was well to bind
the children of Ham
according to the manifest will of God.

This biblical balm was peculiar
in that for centuries
it stilled the conscience of worshippers
as it forged, in churchly furnace
the smelted sword of slave hunters
who corralled generations-
into a new breed, not yet man
since only three fifths, becoming
by Compromise
the remaining two fifths, undone
simian, beast of burden?

Fetters, two forms he observed
shackles of the body
that tether the slave to the master
in chattel, to trade as was needed
mortgaged sold gifted and willed.
And shackles of the mind
hitching the slave to the savage
who becomes the reason for his enslavement,
forever rooted to the plantation

the slave owner his master.
There were some such as these
Informants of Stono, Gabriel Prosser, Nat Turner
Denmark Vesey.

How is chattel explained to a child?
Is he taken to the fields
where the ox and mules are yoked to the plough
to be told, he is kin?
That the God who knows all has cast him in servitude
forever in the shadow of the master?
He asks, *This a benevolent God,*
who sanctions evil to his purpose?
Then I will take flight, he says.

Rebels chance on ways to flee
to break free of bondage
even in death.
At six years old, he enters a portal
Into the written world of words
led by his Mistress, Sarah Auld
but soon debarred further entry by his Master.

If to educate a slave was akin to taboo
then it must be magical, he thought.
It was a telling moment
imperative, the key to the doorway.
He set his mind to discover the magic of freedom.
He will use it to hammer his way in
to loosen the fetters
of this mind-body prison.

At such an early age,
an epiphany
a flash of insight, the lightning rod
that altered the trajectory of his mind
into a new direction.
He seizes upon knowledge for dear life
vowing to stay the course
for to deviate is to betray the self.
It was haunting in nature.
It would not leave him alone.
Everything done was to its purpose.

First there is the enlightenment.
Then the rendering in pursuit of the written word
to grasp any chance to scribble or scrawl
to clip a page on the run
or pocket a snippet of newspaper
later to examine.
The trunk of a tree, his slate
the smooth surface of a pillar, his tablet
a lopsided post, to jot
chalked letters here and there.

Maybe the birthing of a Jeremiad
occurs with words that penetrate,
and missiles that crack the ceiling of apathy.
That word *abolition,* for Douglas
was a revelation.
It had an essence of freeing
that others knew the evils of slavery

apart from himself.
He was not alone,
words can take you on a journey into the future-
set you to dreaming.

For Douglas was a born prophet,
not in the mystical tea leaves reading of the future
but of one who can stir up the settled dust of apathy,
of evil in the present, a call for change.
Few men rivalled him in intelligence
a sage today cast in the light of Jermiah.
He is relevant now as he was then.

Nightingale
(to the memory of Yolanda Barber)

At times her voice is a trailing vine
that binds her in
and hems her spirit.

Then her song echoes through ages
to join the chorus of those
yoked to the hull.

Other times her voice weaves patterns
that promise freedom for generations to come
when the caged bird will break loose
from servitude
to rise above the dirt and dinge
of abject poverty.

Once I heard her when she was provoked.
Then her voice was testy and deep
descending into a contralto gorge
which burst forth
loud in melody
to proclaim-
I am woman
I am strong!

2
Landscape

Taxi Ride to the Beach

At the Mount Hope exit
to the Solomon Hochoy Highway,
I took the Green-band maxi taxi
heading for the deep south
through two worlds-
the new and the old.

New world allure of freshly paved asphalt
multi-laned and arrow-straight
like the Autobahn
with its heedless and daredevil charm,
draws my driver into hopscotching
from lane to lane
gaining-reaching-passing,
with alacrity
as the fervor of a cheetah in pursuit
or the Peregrine falcon's swoop.

I scramble for a secure foothold
lurching from side to side
willing the muscles in my chest to relax.
I duck and weave in my seat
at passing vehicles
which in a split-second swerve suddenly
to avoid a collision.

Unexpectedly, without warning,
the old-world steps in-
dropping precipitously into deep potholes.
Welcome to Coladora!

The sign to the village reads.
The freeway takes on the semblance of a bridle path
where the bitumen gives way begrudgingly
to the underlying gravel bed.

It snakes and twists around the coastline.
I look to my left where it dips into a valley
of galvanized roof tops
rusting from sea blast.
To my right-
the narrow entry to the front door of houses
in a tug-of-war with the pavement
for legroom.

My taxi driver now pilots his vehicle
like the captain of a skiff
riding the crests and troughs.
The road crimps and furrows
mirroring the rise and fall of the waves
in the far distance.

Beneath the misty brine
trickling down on the asphalt
to pockmark its way into a lunar landscape
the road, finally surrenders
with a sinuous curve
meandering to a taper
to reach the shore.

I arrive on a wing and a prayer!

Tropical Storm

Strong winds mimic the mood of
angry skies
above tropic islands
of rugged terrain.
Deep valleys
on the descent,
hail the warm air rising,
to meet the clouds,
moistened by trickling
brooks and streams
coursing their way to the sea.
Cumulus clouds -
pendulous and drooping lazily,
hang over forested peaks
of mountain ranges
ready to burst into a deluge
that would bring forth clapping thunder,
growling resoundingly,
striking terror into the hearts of children.
The Old folks claim that
God and the devil fighting again.
His authority over
the cowering Beelzebub
is complete.
Frightened into docility
by the ancient Cedar
falling to the earth,

Landscape

snapping like a twig,
he flees to Eden's Garden
to seek solace in the serpentine ring.

Market Scene

Once when my sister visited me in Pittsburgh
she brought a painting from home
of the open-air market in Port of Spain.

It hangs on a wall
in my living room
facing an open window.

On mornings
a shaft of light slides through the blinds
to enliven the scene-
of a bustling haggling flow
of eager shoppers
in search of a bargain.

The sun's rays caress the shoulders
of a woman bending over
to lay her vegetables and ground provision
in tidy heaps.
She is dressed in tropical colors
of red and green, with a yellow head tie.

At night the low light bounces off the walls
to frame a quiet scene
of spent labor
and its acceptance.

From time to time,
when I am overcome with loneliness
and the newness of the strange has faded,
I crave the familiar.

Landscape

I look to this painting for comfort
for it speaks to me in the language of colors
and sounds.

I hear the patois spoken
in the background,
the Steelband music
from a portable radio.
I hear the loud laughter
of family gatherings
and of children singing
the old nursery rhymes.
Ring Around the Rosie
Head, Shoulders, Knees and Toes
Mosquito 1, Mosquito 2
London Bridge is Falling Down.

I can see the drifting clouds
hastening towards the sunset,
the hibiscus closing its petal doors
for the night.
I see the crowded streets
of Port of Spain
and the throng of workers
making their way home
at the end of the day.

This painting evokes memories
of people and landscape.
It is a hug,
a handshake
a kiss on the cheek
a reminder of roots.

Song

When I am home in Trinidad, the calls of the Kiskadee and the crowing rooster usher in the new day. These are the sounds I hear upon rising. They are so much an aspect of this tropical island where I was born. When I think of Trinidad, these are two of the many sounds I hear in the recesses of my mind that relocate me back on the island, even though I may be thousands of miles away.

The Kiskadee's monotone is so strident as to occupy a place in my memory that follows me from shore to distant shore. His call, more than any other bird-song fuels my recollection of landscape and traditions. It is why I chose to include a poem in this collection dedicated to this most boisterous and exuberant flycatcher. Among the birds of the island of Trinidad, the Kiskadee seems to insinuate its will and to insist that I pay tribute to its majesty.

In stark contrast to the Kiskadee is the call of the Picoplat, a specie of seed eating finches. The male delivers a very attractive song which includes trills, whistles and chirps. Like the Kiskadee, the distribution is widespread throughout South America and Trinidad and Tobago. However, these birds are almost extinct in Trinidad because of the caged-bird trade.

Growing up in a rural village in Trinidad, I often witnessed caged-bird competitions, where on street corners and in back yards, men would gather to test which bird had a more lasting and melodious song. This practice continues to this day, driving up the demand for songbirds which are now brought in through an illegal trade from Venezuela and other South American countries.

The Kiskadee has escaped this fate due to its less attractive call. It survives to warn us of our indifference to the natural world as it bellows from its high perch--

Kis-ka-dee, Kis-ka-dee!

Watch your step! Watch your step!

Island of Color

Anvil-shaped Trinidad
anchored in the turbulent moody swirl
of the ocean
bears the onslaught of the rolling tide
in its daily rush
towards her receiving shores.

The ruddy light of dawn
floats through tropical gardens
to touch into existence
new blossoms
of hibiscus and heliconia.

Mid-day piercing rays
set up a dancing shimmering whirlpool of heat
heralding the downpour of tropical rain
crackling and splattering
on galvanized roofs.

Ebb tide,
her breakers calm down
on the Western shore
as the distant horizon
dons an orange-pink-yellow
multicolored coat
shadows casting
 on Asphalt gray, zigzagging roads.

Colored rainbow houses,
of bluesy-greens
with magenta tones

light up the faces of buxom beauties
as they casually stroll
or sashay along the pathways.

Each day my Island of color
greets the daily explosion
of light and shade
as the slant of the sun's rays
creates a calabash of color
pouring out its opulence
onto the earth.

I Know Why the Kiskadee Sings

Kiskadee calls out in a shrill voice
piercing the silence at the crack of dawn.
Kis- ka- dee!
Kis Ka dee!

His call, to Rise and Shine!
Rise and Shine!
cuts through the yawning stillness
with razor-edged sounds.

Stylish in a *cosquelle* garb,
King flycatcher dons an eye patch
like the Lone Ranger in a brownish-yellow cape.

He sits on his leafy throne to rule the roost.
Furtively, he sallies out to pounce in mid-hover,
or to snatch in a downward dive
an unwary prey.

As the town crier,
always prying with a nebby nose
Kiskadee commands us –
Look at me!
Look at me!
Kis- ka-dee! Kis-ka dee!

His boisterous squarks
echo through woodlands
stifling the soft warble
of the Picoplat-

Trinidad's songbird
caged to extinction.

Picoplat's melodious chirp
of Chu-chu-chu-chu-wee
Chu-chu-chu-chu-wee
climbs the octave ladder
to delight.

Kiskadee flits and flutters
all day long in a courting dance
from his perch deep in the valley-
where the sun peeps through the canopy-
so furtive and coy.

Often Kiskadee takes to rebuking-
like the priest, with a loud -
Watch you step!
Watch your step!
Kis-ka-dee! Kiss-ka-dee!

Kiskadee mourns the destruction
of his nesting brush
that burns willy-nilly,
and the cool river waters
strangled with debris-
slowly inching along.

From a branch overhanging the waterfall
Kiskadee looks down on the ravine
coursing steadily towards the sea-
as it gathers brightly colored waste-

in magenta, orange and yellow-
colors of the rainbow-wash
from industry-
rushing to meet the coral reef.

I Know why the Kiskadee sings
words are too much like the wind
carried along with the breeze
unheeded and lost in time.

So maybe the birdsong's call
from sun-up to sun-down-of
Watchyourstep!
Watchyourstep!
Kiskadee kiskadee!
would pierce the dullness of apathy
to save this earth-
under the bowl of stars.

My First Snow

Snow,
snow everywhere.
on the rooftops,
in the trees,
in the alleys,
in every nook and cranny,
stuffed into byways,
against retaining walls
backed up against fences
piled high on footsteps,
crammed into crevices
blocking entrances
sequestered out of view
into cul-de-sacs,
all willy-nilly and makeshift.

Children troweling and tunneling
digging and channeling
burrowing and shoveling
scooping out igloos
building caves and castles
mounds and ridges
piled precariously high
teetering and threatening
to tumble into a blanket.

My mind wonders to a place
green and humid
humming with birds and Monarchs

on their migratory winter escape
I am sidetracked.
In an instant
I slip and slide
along the pavement
with outstretch arms to keep my balance
but my shallow-grooved shoes
skid and slither without traction.
I lurch,
recovering
I thread carefully
penguin-style
flat footed,
waddling
short-stepping
shuffling in a rocking roll
up the slushy slope
to my door
spent of breath.

Fall Leaves

The trees in autumn are in a festive mood.
See how with a gust, their extended limbs
wave excitedly in the breeze?
They are dressed in seasonal hues
of energetic orange and vibrant yellow
with a broad sash of passionate red.

Each Fall, nature's canvas springs to life
in a multicolored coat of earth tones
with hints of bronze,
a vivid palette
to paint an abstract scene.

This carnivalesque splendor
has but a short space of time to celebrate.
Then unfolds the winter's tableau of whites and greys.
In protest, the autumn leaves flee the festive scene
to be deposited helter-skelter
crushed beneath our feet.

The trees pull me outdoors
just to look up and wonder at their majesty.
I take a narrow path along a wooded track
where the trees stand tall as sentinels on both sides.
They enclose me in a world suffused
with vitality.

Beneath my feet
the color wheel of Fall foliage, piled high
spins a melody in a minor key
as my steps crunch out the chords.

I lie on a leafy bed
to view this autumn show
hailing each floating leaf
into its resting place
on face and arms and feet.

At peak foliage, I join in the frolic
leaping to the sky
to plunge into a sea of leaves.
Then I am one with Mother nature
nestled in her womb
cut from the same cloth-
indistinct.

Caged Bird

What of the plight of Trinidad's songbirds-
the Picoplat and Semp-
slowly vanishing
into a flight of extinction?

Ripped from their natural habitat,
their sweet songs,
once, part of the landscape
wafting in the breeze
flowing through the plains
now, seldom heard.

I once saw a Semp trapped.
Its slender limbs anchored in *laglee*.
Its delicate feet locked in the thick viscous gum
tapped from the breadfruit tree
and mounted on a thin *Cocoyea* rod.

This trap
blended in with the landscape.
It snuffed the trill of the wabbler
so liquid and pure.

The Semp, unaware
caught in a hop-
hopping on the *Cocoyea* rod
to reach the ripened banana
struggled to free himself,
sank deeper into the snare.

In his wiry cage he darted
from wall to wall
bouncing
in a desperate attempt at freedom.
No longer would he delight in the early morning feed,
flitting from grove to grove of ripened fruit,
or rest on the vein of the banana leaf
to sip the remnants of morning dew.

One early morning as the sun slowly crept
over the crest of the ridge,
adding color to the tapestry of the sky,
I rescued a Picoplat, from its caged world.
I held it gently in my hand as I mounted
the low-lying hill, of its natural habitat.

There stood a lofty Silk Cotton tree
tall and majestic.
I released him to the untamed sweep of the plain
but he kept falling back to earth.
He had lost his wings.
He could no longer fly,
his caged world had removed him from the wild
and had robbed the wild
out-of-him!

El Dorado Village

On those winter days
when I crave the warmth of my native sun
I think of El Dorado,
the village, where my first steps
still carry impressions in the sand-
if only in my mind.

My village, my home
clothed in the verdant garment
of the tropics
beneath an azure sky
is a stone throw
from the aquamarine water
of the breakers' white foam
on the shores of Maracas Bay.

I can smell the aroma of sweet yellow plums,
the ripened sapodillas and guavas,
fruits which lure the macaw
on their morning feeding frenzy
cloaked in a cacophony of sounds.

Home is the lingering traces of scent
sounds, that follow me from place to place.
A trail in my mind,
which can surface at odd moments
in a Proustian realm
without warning.

Home is fluid-protean
like the shifting sands-unfixed,
as turbulent as the Caribbean Sea.
It cannot be contained in time.
It morphs and flows.
There is no entrance or exit
into a definite experience of home.
The landscape changes by the minute.
The patois mutates ever so slightly,
that within a short space of absence
you will not be recognized or understood.
I sometimes fear
that the soft underbelly of my mind
would cease to recall this place
where my navel-string is buried.

Paramin

Some days cumulous clouds climb slowly
through the skyscape
to caress the façade
of brick houses fastened with mortar
resting on stilts on a mountainous ledge.

Paramin, sprawling along the cliff's top,
threatens to slide into the surrounding valley.
The road to the village
snakes around the side of the hill
rising in an uphill sweep
to descend in roller coaster style-
with tight turns and swift drops.

Maxi-taxis ply the route
in a frenetic haste all-day
scaling the edge of the cliff,
to take villagers or eager visitors on a journey
which is a test of mettle.
I sat up-front with the driver,
bobbing and weaving
as I lurch from side to side in my seat.

But with smooth dexterity,
my driver, with untroubled composure
and adhering to the tacit law of the road-
to always yield to an oncoming vehicle
where the road tapers
brings us to the mountain top

or the valley below
safe and sound!

The Poui Tree

The children of El Dorado Village
delight in the season
of the flowering Poui.

They wait patiently beneath the trees
for a strong flurry to waft through the branches.
They yearn for the release of strewn blossoms
cascading through the air,
to carpet the earth,
and cling to their upturned faces.

With a strong gust
they frolic and dance
adorned in a mantle of bright yellow blooms
against their dark skin.
They parade with leis of trumpet-shaped flowers
around their slender necks and wrists.

Once Raleigh in search of gold
the fable told
espied the flowering Poui
on a range of golden covered hills,
far off in the distance
as he approached land by sea.

The Poui beckoned to him
to pay homage
to its golden flower splendor.
He thought he had found El Dorado,
but the flowering Poui
with the semblance of a golden city

from afar
in full florescence
confused his pioneering greed.

Still every year the Poui trees blossom
and the children of El Dorado Village welcome
the season once again
to rejoice in their splendor.

Full Moon

Caribbean full moon
 guides me to the cove
where I sink into
the warm bay
flecked with silver moonbeams.

Later, I rise like Oshun the Yoruba goddess
out of the water.
My path is lit by the moon
full in a tropic sky
gleaming on the sugarcane storks.
The crest of Immortelle trees
tower above with sheltering arms
over the cocoa trees beneath.

I espy
a strand of moonbeam
seeping through the canopy
to touch cocoa pods
hanging from the ashen trunk
like a necklace of beads
purple in the moonlight.

An errant glow spreads across galvanized roofs
of patchwork houses
perched precariously on wooden stilts.
The village is asleep
unaware that once the ancients used
the afterglow to hunt and court,

to sit circle-wise
and recite the creation stories
that gave us the myths
we hold dear.

Then the brake of dawn
disrupts the magic
as full moon in a night sky
looming high above the mountain range
slides slowly into the skyline
and disappears.

Leatherback
(for the Nature Seekers of Matura)

> Custodians in their nightly vigil
> patrol Matura Beach in Trinidad
> to protect the ancient mariner of the seas.
> She is quarry when out of her watery world,
> at risk, in the pangs of labor.
>
> The one-ton lute-shape leviathan
> plies through water with ease
> yet struggles on shore to dig her nest.
> With flat front flippers like oars in troubled waters
> she pulls hard
> pauses, then pulls again to advance
> in less than her length.
> The warmth of the tropical sun
> trapped in the sand will incubate her eggs.
>
> Under the late moonlight
> Nature Seekers of Matura
> line the shore in a conservation space.
> Once they were poachers
> leaving behind a graveyard of discarded parts
> for the carrion.
> Prized as a delicacy
> eggs traveling down her oviduct
> back then, landed in hands
> eager to boost the libido.

    Nature's course is hazardous.
Her newly hatched babies
hurrying towards the horizon
pass through a minefield
of waiting crabs and shorebirds.
In the water, they become fodder
for an army of sharks, squids and cuttlefish.
Yet the leatherback has survived the dinosaurs.

Nature Seekers of Matura know the threat
but their reach ends at the shore line.
The hatchling they saved today
may be the adult snagged tomorrow
among floating pieces of fishing net
or tangled in fishing line
or tied up in an odd ball
to sink lower and lower,
pulled down by its own weight to drown.
The odds of survival,
one in a thousand.

Sea Bathing

Gliding into the frothy carpet
of the spent wave,
the current drags me towards the breakers.
I brace myself for the onslaught of the rollers
as I climb the crests of the waves,
the floating kelp ropes clinging to my neck.

The ebb and flow of the tides
set up an ageless rhythm
never changing its tempo
punctual and ceaseless.
A slow drawing and unfolding
like breathing
without a care in the world,
with time to spare.

It did not match my breath
shallow, hurried, in a rush
sometimes impatient
like a candle lit at both ends
because life is so short.

In the watery hall
adorned with wild coconut
and sea lavender
I tread to keep astride
if only for a moment.
The lash of the waves tosses me
like flotsam towards the shore.
The force is mean and swift

without respect of persons.
King Xerxes thought he could punish the sea
by whipping it into shape
and poking it with hot irons.
Still, it continued to reap havoc with his plans.

Then I rise up out of the water
like a crushed nymph
with a crown of sea grapes
clad in a raiment of sand.

Sundrops

At first Spring
in anticipation
I often listen to the weather forecast
for clear skies and a sunny day.

The early Spring thaw brings promise
of a splash of color
to satiate my yearning
for the delightful Sundrops'
showy bright yellow primrose.

Each morning
I would bend over
to inspect the buds.
But they resolve to be cloistered,
hidden and shy
in a tight knob
refusing to unfold.

Sundrops thirst for the tropic heat.
In winter they lie torpid
to hide in hibernal solitude.
The stamen and pistil
resting in dormancy
to await the advent of Spring,
and a season of fecundity.

Once when the conditions were ideal-
with penetrating sunshine

in a Caribbean flair,
they remained secluded.

But on a cold and gloomy day
with heavy moisture and a light drizzle.
I tarried all morning indoors
certain the Sundrops would not appear.

But behold!
There they emerged
in all their incandescent glory,
bright and yellow on a dreary day.
This is divinity!
A golden lining beneath a dark cloud.

3
Mindscape

Eutierria

At this late stage,
I crave unity with nature.
I have taken to tending flowers
in a desperate need to touch beauty
to find delight in the budding rose
that unwittingly shares its splendor
in its own good time.

Standing amongst working bees
busily gathering nectar
I see no conflict,
no vying for position,
no jostling or shoving
just harmony and rhythm.

Aspiration has dampened my muse.
Ambition has fettered my senses
to see and smell and hear the good earth.
I shudder at stillness and the flow inwards
not knowing that poems are sired
in the womb of silence.

I am tired of keeping steps with the world-
the urgency to achieve
the constancy of endeavor
in which failure is no option.

My orderly world of computation and logic
frowns on happenstance

that decries nature's mercurial ways
and uncertain temperament.

But in the mercurial
such wonders abide!
I imagine a world without sound-
no color or contrast
no thoughts or tongues
all fingerprints the same
everyone identical.

And I long to shed the veil
between myself and the world of consequence
to pair with nature
in her vastness
where my seeing mind
can temporarily filter through
into insight.

 No longer would I question my mortality
but accept it as nature's way of transitioning
to a new habitat
full of wonder.

The Immigrant's Fear

I am aware of a thin thread of foreboding
always with me in my waking hours
that often creeps into repose.
This feeling of disquiet
will not allow me to lose track of origin
of connection to place
where there still resides
kith and kin.

Always, I am mindful of distance-
of separation,
where even though I am a settler in a new place
I have never completely left the old.
That, every long-distant call could be of sad tidings
and the request to return
before it's too late.

I live in readiness
always to expect the unexpected.
I wear the cloak of trepidation
as an aspect of the migrant.

My circumstance gives shape to a form of stoicism
to cover my anxiety.
This unease, I dare not share
due to my upbringing of many years
living under the British gaze
that epitomizes the stiff upper lip-
where to show emotion is to admit defeat.

For in this era-
in this modern place where I have settled-
"The quality of mercy" is "strain'd."
I wear the wide grin as a shield,
for it guarantees safety against
the scorn of apathy.

Exemplar

The elderly Chinese peanut vendor
was always under the Saman tree in the village,
constant, unvarying in purpose
steady and reliable.
I could count on him for my salt nuts.
None of his children sold peanuts.
From the slow drip of pennies into the bucket
he paid for their education abroad
in the professions.
Even today when I waver from resolve
I hear his voice from the past calling-
"Nuts, Nuts, get your peanuts,
salt nuts, fresh nuts, roast nuts."
We never knew his name
so, we called him the Nuts man.
He taught me perseverance.

The Syrian merchant came by on Saturdays
driving a ramshackle beat-up Ford pickup
stacked with bales, boxes and bottles
to sell to poor mothers on credit.
After many years of wayfaring
he built a corporation.
We did not know his name
so, we called him the Syrian man.
He taught me aspiration.

The East Indian man who rode a bicycle
sounded a horn every morning.
He sold *Doubles* out of a biscuit tin-

curried Channa, sandwiched between
fried pieces of dough.
One day the sound of the horn ceased.
He had opened up a restaurant in Port of Spain.
We did not know his name
so, we called him the *Doubles* man.
He taught me to dream.

The Black woman at the corner of Green Street
sold coconut-
soft, medium and hard jelly
and coconut water from the nut.
One day she figured out how to diversify
this elixir of good health, by bottling it.
Today it is in the grocery shops.
We did not know her name
so, we called her the Coconut woman.
She taught me to be resourceful.

My role models are earth-bound
moral and sensual folk,
shaping the meager into abundance,
of means and spirit.
The chronicle of their lives
now serves as my own living epistle
I dwell upon to fortify me
whenever I falter.

Proustian

I rely on small serendipities,
chance encounters to soothe my nostalgia
living in this new place of four seasons.

One day, I walked into a grocer's shop
in the heart of South Philadelphia.
The air was filled with the fragrance of ripened guavas.

Suddenly, I was riding an olfactory wave
through time and space
to a place where the scent of guavas
fills the air.

I hear the parrots flying overhead
aiming for the grove
with their loud chatter.

I am back in anvil-shaped Trinidad
descending on a cloud of aroma
into the village of El Dorado,
where at eight or ten years old
I am a tomboy.

I am suspended on a limb
high up on a plum tree
wedged between a fork, trapped
no way forward
can't go backward
but determine to debunk the stereotype
of frailty to the village boys.

I fall.
Nursing a deep gash on my leg, I rise
hobble home, dry-eyed and smug.
Then without warning
the moment dissipates
as I touch my battle scar.

First

That night in New York my cultural eyes
looked down from the sixth floor of the hotel
and saw rain.

I wondered about the hatless crowd
walking unaware
some bald-pated to catch the streaming drizzle.

In my mind's scenic landscape
no record of falling snow existed.
So, I saw rain
and wondered.

Then lightly it floated aimlessly
to rest on the window sill
flake by flake
and I marveled at nature's way.

Opera
To Sally Michalski

I see a wall of white faces
when I am in the Opera Hall.
I represent the missing few
whose stories in Opera are not told.

The gate keepers at the Met,
faithfully safeguard the canon-
a fortress built by
Verdi, Wagner, Stravinsky, Puccini and others
to keep the hoi polloi at bay
from flipping the libretto
to allow sharing the domain.

Black singers long to sing of love and loss
in their own skin,
to unravel life in our own time
not of a European eighteen century world.

The power of urgency
drives the impulse to stay the course.
For decades the forebearers have chipped
at the icy response to their talents.
Beginning with the works of
Guadeloupe-born-of-a slave,
Chevalier Saint George, the Black Mozart.
His operas and symphonies
from sheer beauty
could not be kept down.

After years of obscurity,
he is back in vogue.

Witness the pantheon of virtuosos
Black and American
whose works were debarred entry,
or submerged under a mountain of rejection-
John Thomas Douglas, William Grant Still
Henry Lawrence Freeman's opera *The Octoroon*
the Met claimed-
"We do not see our way clear to accept this work."

Yet there is Porgy and Bess
known as the "First great American opera."
Premiered at the Met in 1985.
It's fraught history of stereotyping
adapted from a story told by an onlooker-outsider
with an improbable eulogy in song by Porgy,
naïve and simple
"I got plenty o' nuttin and
nuttin's plenty for me."

What few black composers of opera
have been allowed access
display an array of color and tone
in an amazing lyrical harmony
using African percussion accents.
(I am thinking of Anthony Davis and Terrance Blanchard).
Combining the music of American Jazz
with a classical score,
the percussive dance of Black fraternal Stepping

as featured in *Fire Shut Up in My Bones*
to tell an American story,
unconventional in form and musical complexity.

The Opera landscape
is replete with talented composers
male and female,
waiting for a chance
to stage their operas.
I have a CD in my collection
The Unknown Flower,
by Charsie Randolph Sawyer,
a soprano whose voice weaves a silken thread
up and down the octave loom
to unveil a splendid tapestry
of music by Black female composers
of classical music.

It has opened up a world for me
and set me thinking
of Harry Burleigh and Dvorak.

What would classical music in America be today
if they had listened to Dvorak's words?
He suggested merging jazz harmonies
with the many colors and tones,
the cut and thrust of the spirituals
and the moaning of the Native chants
to create an American classical tradition
apart from Europe.

In 1892?
No less a pipe dream of sorts!

On Imagination

Queen of vision
imperial and resplendent
enters unimpeded
into the sphere of the creator,
a place far-flung
an empyrean domain
where angelic praises
proclaim thy wonders.

Imagination!
You in flight, soar like an eagle
riding on a floating stream
to capture the song of the universe
to tumble through the celestial realm
with a giant leap among the stars
world to world.

Imagination!
Invention's source
province of the creative impulse
fount of music and art,
the root of drama
genesis of the word.

Imagine
a universe without flair,
plain and drab
untouched by the hand of insight
as the primordial soup

devoid of variety
bereft of form.

For what hope to dream
without fancy's escort,
but with resignation
curl inward into a barren coil of torpid space
to languish.

Would creation shed a tear
for lack of novelty
where all is tame
and brightened morn darkens?
Or would she leap for joy
in bountiful array?

Assisted Living

The old woman said
they laughed at her
because she has a heavy accent.
She has no friends.
It is a place that mirrors society-
color lines, class lines, sexism and
homophobia.

In her decrepitude, solitude is vast.
She feels her worth
in her declining years questionable.

She bumps into people
barely seeing through her cataracts.
In the bewilderment of senility,
she dreads complaining.
She hates to be a bother
for fear of reprisal.

The passing of time is different.
It treads slowly
not like the good old days
when it galloped.
In the early years
when she was full of bustle
and life was a flurry
she would often say to herself-
"Where did the day go
or the month or the year."

Now she gets lost
in the unhurried rendering of time.

She does not understand
the new slang.
Her repeated questions
annoy young folks.
They suspect the onset of Alzheimer.
So, she retreats inwards
locking herself up inside herself.
Once in a while, lucidity comes in waves.

Of the five senses she once had
she is left with-
two, maybe three?
She tries to be useful
but she just gets in the way.
The only thing that connects her
to the then is-
the lyrics of the old songs.
She can sing them in perfect pitch without falter
but she cannot remember
what she had for supper.

At her advanced age
she is still plagued by desire
a sort of dull ache
that threatens to engulf her.
Her libido is slow to be tamed
still primitive and urgent at times
she is a tigress in heat again,
as when at thirty.

She has no use for this primordial instinct
a bequest for human survival
that continues to rack her mind
while her body is frail and teetering.
She longs to return it to its Maker
but it threatens to cling on to the very end
a wasteful and impractical drive.
So much for evolution!

To a Genius

This drive you were born with
clamors for release.
It is at the helm of your waking
the overlord of your actions,
directing the care of your gift.
It created the mold
that shaped the outcome
of your talent.

You are the chosen to be envied,
but to you it is an affliction
a trial,
an ordeal for which there is no release.
It consumes you, this fire
that sets you apart from everyone
and makes a recluse of your ways.

For you are a genius.
Such as you have moved mankind along.
But at what price?

You are the sacrificial lamb.
This cup cannot be taken away!

Bebop

Bebop uses the power of rhythm
to capture sound waves for its own design
through tight strands of rhythm.

Within this matrix of fast tempo,
rapid chord changes,
instrumental mastery,
is freedom to fashion
forge, and frame.

Each tune
is occasion to reshape the melody
never to play the same refrain twice.
For here lies the essence of Bop,
its dais, the bandstand
where it can reach heights
not experienced elsewhere.

Bop molds vibrations
Into harmony
that somewhere in the sphere
riding on the waves of sound
musicians meet
to experience the potency of the beat.

In the flow of the rhythm
they connect with what they play.
They are in the zone, confident
locked, unaware of the audience,
pleasure no longer from a sea of faces
but, from the power of music.

Yes! Freedom is in Bop's complex harmonies
with timely reference to the melody,
as the horns and piano improvise along the scale
with the tempo-keeping drums,
to play this music-
the way it is meant to be played!

The Road Well-Traveled

I wondered-
if from young
they were inseparable,
childhood sweethearts
or best friends,
maybe neighbors.
Was she, the girl next door?
Did he ask her to the prom?

For a while they walked together
but then she took the road well-traveled
not wanting to reinvent the wheel
but to enjoy
a quiet cozy trail
without fanfare.
For at heart
she was a home girl
seeped in the ways of daily vespers
and bible verses
to catch a cleric.

But he set his eyes on adventure
on the road less traveled
with few footprints to step into
sometimes a path uncharted
without signpost
that led to the frontier.

Often, she thought of him
his dare-devil, swashbuckler ways
and wondered how he fared.
But the road less traveled
soon led to a cul-de-sac
of truncated hopes
that robbed him of the will
to fashion a new path.

The pot of gold evaded his grasp-
for with each forward step to reach the rainbow
it kept receding
being an illusion.
Within one season
he found and lost the allure of Eros
and after many moons
bone-tired and weary
he retraced his steps
to the old homestead
where life was predicable
and the roads paved
of the tried and true.

There, the girl next door
still snug in her homely ways
welcomed him to share the ride
on the road well-traveled.

Cancer Ward
(For Teresa Render)

My friend has cancer.
She said, "I want you to know what's going on."
Her tone, casual, in control
knocking the promontory of fear
down to her size
which for me the Big C spawns,
I said, "Are you ok?
Am with you all the way."
She replied, "Oh yea, I'll be fine."

In the cancer ward
there are no beds.
High backed recliners face smart TVs
ensconced in private cubicles.
No one looks ill.
Chemo drips lazily into a port near her collarbone
as we talked about summer blooms,
her capricious Siamese
and how to make Gazpacho.

Later in the day
we climbed the sloping hills nearby
as a gust of wind played with her hair
which once was shoulder length.
She said, "this is not new for me,
I wore it like this once."

The march of modern medicine
slowly tempers the lash of despair for her
often linked to the big C.
She finds support in a community of patients
proudly displaying her certificate
of completion with chemo
a therapy without discernment
of good and bad cells.
There is damage to her liver and sinuses.

Her confidence is the weapon she brandishes daily.
She is a warrior for life
not content to settle at the way-station
of despondency.
The better days are the ones she dwells upon.

Double Standard

Was Odysseus expected to remain celibate
while fighting the Trojan war?
During his hiatus
his wife Penelope had a hundred suitors
but remained chaste
under close scrutiny.

The exploits of the intrepid warrior,
traveled far and wide.
I wonder how Penelope took to his infidelities.
His famous Nostos, after the war
was a ten-year wandering
of dropping anchor here and there
for some R & R.
At Aeaea, he met the goddess Circe.

Referred to as an enchantress
(what else could she be?).
Her knowledge of potions and herbs
was hardly a hurdle to climb,
for men will sow their wild oats,
to be called a stud, but she?
A slut, no less.

She was a link in the long chain
of female temptresses
in fable and fantasy
extending from Eve
to Homer's Helen
whose abduction is doubtful.

Was it elopement?
Or did she seduce Paris?

The myth of the female mystique-
a sort of wild power
to trap men into indiscretion
is pervasive in our folklore.
Sirens and mermaids are female
Delilah, Salome, Jezebel
they entice men to their death.

Witches are burnt.
Are wizards?
This imagined untamed, fierce power
ascribed to the female
is the fulcrum, the axis
upon which the imbalance rests.
Who opened Pandora's box?
Whose curiosity killed the cat?
She, by her very nature
is blamed for the double standard.

In the fictitious world of cinema,
men and women in power act differently.
The male, dispassionate
hardcore, hell-bent.
The female, shrewish, angry
scheming, with feminine wiles
to entrap.

  Shakespeare's Cleopatra
painted as the archetype femme fatale

as having taken a leaf from Deliah's book
uses her beauty and charm
in a mesh of sexual allure.
Firstly, to regain her position as queen of the Nile
with help from Caesar
then from Anthony in hopes of annexing Rome.

She bore children by each of them.
Was this purely altruistic
to save her country from domination
or was it self-seeking?

Flourishing throughout the centuries,
seeping down the ages
within art and Literature
Keates-*La Belle Dame sans Merci*
in the origin stories-Adam and Eve
is an attempt to bridle female sexuality
by the creation of myth and tropes.

Today the vamp is here to stay.
Her air of mystification
has been elevated to high society art
in the operas of Bizet's Carmen
Saint-Saens' Samson and Deliah
staged at the Met.

No less!

Leaving Home

It was not for want of ease
that I took leave of kith and kin
from those familiar stomping grounds
where everyone knew my name.

I craved new ways of mastery
to cradle erudition
and to unfurl the jaundiced way of thinking
insular, narrow, provincial.

I entered the metropolis
beyond the horizon
to extend the reach of the island's
circumscribed
inward looking view of discernment
confined by the skyline.

I sought to relinquish
those ideals I once embraced
unrealistic and irrelevant
to slowly dismantle the shrine
held in reverence
which then ambushed me into
defeat and pessimism.

In this new place
beneath the comfort of another sun
my hope is for new perspectives-
a new outlook

a broader way of thinking
the raiment of confidence
and esprit de corps.

The Silent

They sat around in the hotel lobby,
twenty or more baby boomers.
I could feel their animation.
I sensed the emotion
on faces aglow with pathos,
and eyes of laughter, humor,
or their curled lips of dread and ridicule.

I watched them
engaged in conversation
of years gone by and life's vicissitudes.
Of marriages, divorces and death,
children and grand.
Of travel and countries
strange cultures
and bizarre foods
and Andrew Zimmern.

Of the old movies
with Liz Taylor, Monroe, Gable and Mitchum,
of the Presidents and change-
"Yes, We Can!"
The wars-Vietnam, in particular
Haight Ashbury and the Flower People.
They talked well into the wee hours of the morning
yet not a sound was heard.
Only the graceful movements
of their fingers
as they signed to each other.

On Returning

I was returning home after a long hiatus
of nurturing a seed-
a tiny slip of a dream
which in my mind started as an afterthought
that soon grew in intent and purpose
to dare to aspire and to achieve elsewhere.

Now that I was back on a short visit
I expected the familiar greeting
the neighborly sociable gathering
like birds of a feather…
getting on like a house on fire
like peas in a pod.

I visualized a welcome
as flourishing as the verdant landscape,
burgeoning with joy and laughter
bearing gifts and invitations
anxious to learn of my exploits,
my escapade into the metropolis.
There would be warm embraces
and kisses on the cheek
songs and celebration
preparing the fatted calf.

Then I stepped on shore
and out of the dream.
I recognized an acquaintance.
"You back with us?" She quipped.
"Only for ten days." I said in my careful Trini twang

so as not to sound like a 'fresh-water Yankee'.
"Well, some of us choose to stay to build the country.
Some take their talents elsewhere."

My heart reeled with the censure,
my mind hurled with remorse.
The reproach awakened new wounds of guilt.
I had left to seek my fortunes elsewhere,
now I no longer deserve to be called a native.
I was remiss in my duties to the Motherland.

I was an AWOL

Dawn

From inside the reach of time
deep in the crevice of memory
majestic towers
once surveyed the earth-scape
from their lofty columns.

Earth's forested sentinels-
extended their sweeping limbs
to caress each compass point
unchallenged.

Beneath their shaded wings
of leafy glade
a creation story first unfurled.

Then the age of progress
with a searing thirst
for timber
a flair for felling
Cedar Maple Elm Pine,
usurped the throne
of the Mother-
once a mighty tree fortress
where stood the Angel Oaks.

Now
citified highways bloom and blossom
into byways
tunneling through the subterranean world
of the root cap.

4
CultureScape

Natural Healing

The medicinal properties of plants are beginning to attract attention among scientists and pharmaceutical companies in the developed world. Of the top two hundred prescription drugs in the US, eighty percent are from natural sources. There is a treasure trove of tropical plants inhabiting wild uncultivated places that have become avenues for bio-prospectors. The risk of over harvesting and commercial exploitation is real.

Furthermore, indigenous peoples have relied on nature's pharmacy for thousands of years for their medicinal needs. Over commercialization of medicinal plants and herbs could result in a loss of access to people whose only source of medication is of the traditional. Worldwide, the threat of extinction of plants with medicinal properties is also a concern. Thousands of medicinal plants are in jeopardy of disappearing.

For developing countries such as Trinidad and Tobago on a quest for new natural resources and remedies, the harnessing and revival of ancestral knowledge about traditional medicine could be a gateway leading towards economic benefits and self-sufficiency. Therefore, the need to monitor outside interest in traditional medical supply is of vital importance.

My African and Indian elders have always listened to the earth. They hear her voice clear and loud. Her wisdom is the fountainhead from which springs the ways of healing and wellbeing. Now the sound is muffled by modern ways but traces still linger in the rural villages. The healing properties of nature are lodged deep in the recesses of our collective memory, in the storehouse of our mind. From as early as 1500 BC, ancient Egyptians recorded remedies made from wild and wonderful medicinal plants. The Ebers Papyrus lists eight hundred of these. Medicinal lore cites the healing nature of plants generally growing in uncultivated lots. Infusions and preparations prepared from seeds, bark, flowers and roots to restore balance.

Bush medicine is the colloquial name we in Trinidad give to traditional medicine. It has for many years been part of the cultural landscape with remnants from Amerindian, enslaved Africans and Indian indentured servants. Regardless of the dominance of conventional medicine bush medicine continues to thrive in some communities, those primarily in the remote parts of the island such as Toco and Paramin. The unique proximity of Trinidad to South America contributes to Trinidad's natural medicinal flora.

Whenever I return home, I pay a visit to my friend in the East in a little village called Matelot. She is a bush tea connoisseur who prepares for me a cleansing concoction consisting of purges and laxative which is guaranteed to rid the intestines of toxins. It is a ritual which happens to be a throwback from my early childhood days when my mother would administer a dreadful tea made from the Senna Pod during the school vacation. This was often followed by a dose of castor oil or worm grass tea.

Bush Tea

My mother hung orange peel to dry
from a ledge above her kitchen window.
Once a month, as a newly initiated young lady
I drank a tea of orange peel, and cinnamon
to guide the menstrual flow.

Often, she brewed a cooling drink of Zaboca
and Carilie leaves
laced with ginger, she claims-
to restore the balance
of hot and cold in the body.

In the back yard, a Bacanoe tree
strewed broad dry leaves curled up
like the fist of a giant's hand.
My mother made a tea from its leaves
at the onset of the flu.

At front of the house,
the aromatic scent of fever grass
clung to the air.
When infused with Black Sage and Zebapique
it could cure a dry cough.

Across the road, Nature-
the Master Apothecary
furnished a mecca of medicinal flora-
in an uncultivated plot-
with such a profusion of wild and wonderful plants
like Wonder-of-the-World.

On mornings we drank Lime-bud tea
or Cocoa tea from the grated cocoa pod.
At night Soursop tea to bring on sleep.
Then at the end of the school vacation-
a worm grass and senna purgative.

New mothers after delivery
savored the cooling effect of a bush bath
of Blue Vervain, Neem and Hibiscus-
a restorative of cooling herbs
to heal and balance the womb.

The ubiquitous, sometimes edible herbal weed
almost hugging the ground-
the old people call Plantain
with a blue florescence
was seeped in boiling water
to treat eye problems.

According to the elders-
we owe much to the natural pharmacies of Mother Earth
and the plant crafters of past generations-
those herbalists of Amerindian,
African and Indian folk traditions
with their deft hands
concocting healing remedies
for survival.

Christmas Fare
To Nancy Glover, the Chef

Christmas morning breakfast-
I untie a Pastelle wrapped in banana leaf
to unfold the yellow meaty-filled cornmeal turnover
charged with flavor.
The subtle savor of pimento sends
a jolt of picante and from the capers
a hint of tang.

A few raisins sprinkled, suggest sweetness
to tame the saltiness from the baked ham
coated with *Chow Chow* relish
dabbed with *Sorrel* jelly
to satiate my eager palate.

Lunch is on a whim, until dinner,
the main meal of the day.
Formal and festive, the dinner table
suffused with joie de vivre
is set in merry reds and festive greens,
tempered by demure white touches
of linen napkins and dishes piled high
with the colors of island fare-

Pigeon peas, rice, Macaroni Pie (not Macaroni and Cheese)
traditional 'Ground Provision'-
Dasheen, Yam and Cassava,
Potato Salad (not the American version)
but with beets, colorful peppers, finely chopped onions-
no eggs.

Meat, a leg of pork, baked with pineapple slices
and oven roasted turkey with stuffing.
Sorrel and Ginger Beer on ice.

Later for dessert-
a slice of liquored black rum cake,
the fruit mixture of raisins, sultans, mixed peel,
cherries, and prunes finely macerated and soaked
for months,
with a good rum and Cherry Brandy.
I am captivated by the cake's textured firmness-
not light, like the commonplace sponge cake
but dark and moist.

A glass of *Ponche de Creme's* velvety liqueur
or some homemade Ginger Beer
from raw ginger, grated
seeped with cinnamon and cloves,
sweetened to taste,
adding a dash of Cream of Tartar to "clarify" the liquid,
then bottled and set in the sun to "cure."
It is the drink to compliment
Caribbean's Mother of all cakes-
the Black Cake!

Following Christmas Day's spread-
the days leading up to New Year
are filled with leftovers-
for nothing is sweeter than
good 'ole' *Ma Ca Fourchette!*

Parang Party

That night, *Los Alumnos de San Juan*
with a fast six-eight rhythmical Serenal
was on stage.

From a short distance away,
I felt the pull of the cuatro,
the urge to dingolay
as the Paranderos strummed a rhythm
drawing me in,
closer.

I joined the throng of dancers
stepping into the beat of the box-bass.
The throbbing tempo moving us
forward-backward
forward-backward
me, with arms akimbo,
or flung in the air.
'De' music was so sweet!

The toc-toc woody sound of the claves,
the chac-chac rattling maracas
drove the tempo to a hurried pitch.
Then the fiddles quivered with delight
to lead the voices up the octave ladder
into Rio Manzanares.

I remembered that song
to the river-Manzanares

by the Venezuelan composer-
José Antonio Lopez-
who paid tribute to a river without mercy,
Sin Piedad.

Femicide

To the memory of women such as
Andrea Bharatt, Ashanti Riley and Adeina Alleyne
who have succumbed to femicide in Trinidad and Tobago.

To women such as Melissa Cassim
who have taken a stand against the violence
perpetrated against women
which rivals that of some developed countries.

To the cries of women on the streets of Port of Spain
who demand to be protected, to be safe,
to be able to walk the streets without being harassed.
"To walk free, not brave!" They exclaim.
"Not to be silenced."
Women's lives matter!
For she is the mother, daughter, niece, cousin, sister, aunt.

To the parents, with a fallen child
who are consoled with the words of the old maxim-
Time will heal!
Give it time, time will heal.
"Time will never heal" says the mother of Ashanti,
who waits for the earth to settle on her daughter's grave
before she erects a tombstone.

Deep in the Aripo Valley
where the river hugs the slope
they dumped her daughter's body.
A marker adorned with plastic flowers
points to the spot
where she was found.

Mangled

High up from its lookout
the sharp-eyed sentinel bird of prey-
the Black Corbeau
picks out the mangled form of a woman
spreadeagled-
with steering eyes that cannot see,
dumped in a discarded heap
twisted in a rough shape with limbs
pointing to the cardinal points.

His loud plaintive squawks
mourn the essence of a life
broken and snapped-
toss willy-nilly
over a precipitous gorge
to lodge in a rocky crevice without burial rites
as is the custom.

The raptor,
ascending from his perch to feast upon the form,
crushed into mutilated stillness
is staved off
by the unsettled life-force
shrouded like a mist around her,
impenetrable, foreboding.
He checks the descent of his talons.

The Plight of Bucco Reef

We destroy the fragile beauty of the reef
walking in crepesoled feet among the coral.
We break the limbs off the Staghorn
to trade as souvenirs
to adorn mantles and desks
as we peddle with the tourist.

The Brain coral poisoned with debris and pollution
struggles to release her eggs.
The Star and Elkhorn polyps are stifled by algae
nourished by runoff.

Bucco Reef weeps
for tomorrow's generation.
They will not see through glass-bottom boats
the fragile ecosystem
of coral communities.

To appease our conscience
we masquerade at Carnival each year
in costumes of papier-mâché and rattan
to represent the reef.

But when the parade is over
we dispose of the costumes with abandon
in the nearest river
Bucco is quickly forgotten.

We will remember, though
the plight of Bucco Reef again
at next year's carnival parade.

The Trinidadian Creole

The Trinidadian creole not only developed over centuries of colonization under Spanish, French and British rule, but also acquired words from languages such as Yoruba, Hindustani, Tamil and other South Asian lexicons. The official language is English, having been designated as such in 1823 by the Crown. A new wave of transformation is underway today with the influx to Trinidad of Spanish-speaking Venezuelans, along with their patois. We anticipate further influences on the Trinidadian creole.

Over the years there has been some impact of the Venezuelan culture on the daily life of Trinidadians especially at Christmas time with the musical rhythms of Parang. However, with the massive influx entering Trinidad today, the forecast is for no less than a cultural effervescence, in language, food, dance and religion.

The word *mamaguy* is probably of Spanish origin from the phrase- *mamar gallo* 'to make a monkey off.' The creole is so expressive that sometimes no English word can, at times, best express what we Trinis wish to say. English words can be so dry and pedantic as to downplay the meaning and the full impact of what one is feeling at the moment.

Mamaguism, the noun, is not totally flattery, hyperbole or exaggeration. Neither is it entirely a compliment. It is some of each but there is an undercurrent of deception implicit in mamaguism. Mamaguy, the verb, has at its center, possession. Mamaguism is used by Trinidadian men in the pursuit of a romantic interest. Both men and women in the company of family or friends employ mamaguism as a way of ingratiating themselves or to try to kowtow, or pander to, someone in order to court their approval. Soon to follow would be a request to grant a favor. This could be a request to borrow money or to seek the assistance of the person for any number of reasons.

Mamaguism

Not an absolute lie
No! no!
Some truth then?
Maybe but not entirely.
Oh, you mean flattery,
a pat on the back?

Well, flattery could be transparent
Clear-cut and less seductive.
A pleasant indulgence-
you know it to be tinged
but you wallow a little
wading in its coziness.
Still, it is flattery and you realize it.

But mamaguism is a two-faced imp
tarnished by deceit,
spouting a powerful narcotic-
you want to drink long and deep.
You become ripe for the pickings.
Like the artificial flowers
on the mantle-
not the real McCoy.

Mamaguism says-
to a romantic interest,
"Your face could launch a thousand ships,
like Helen of Troy!"
Or to a family member you have neglected,
"You have found the fountain of youth,

you never age!
You look the same as when I saw you last."
Or, to a casual friend you hope to ask a favor
your initial approach of fawning,
"You sing like a nightingale."
Or to an acquaintance for whom you owe an apology
"You have the patience of Job."

No one is spared from mamaguism.
With a spoonful of truth
a trait can blossom into a rare finding
like the white peacock,

Mamaguism is a boldface lie dressed in velvet
to titillate your fancy.
You are not aware of any ulterior motive,
then out of its hiding place comes a request
for help or handout or forgiveness.
You are at this point ensnared,
you allow yourself this one indulgence.
You fall for it.

To yourself you say-
Mamaguay me!
You throw caution to the wind
While plunging in.

The Patois

The language I live in
cry, castigate myself, celebrate,
I first heard in the womb.

I carry the patois always with me.
A calabash filled with fragments of Wolof
Hausa, Spanish, French
Yoruba, Tshi, Bengali
English, Hindi, Punjabi
words.

The creole creeps in
unannounced,
surreptitiously untangling my moods
comforting,
anchoring me to the ancestors.

Yesterday
out of the din and clatter
of a busy thoroughfare in New York
the patois trickled through
unannounced
sudden-like
flowing like sweet mango juice.

From a spirited tongue
the voice of a Trini
in a cadence that lilt and fall
lilt and fall
like the calypso beat,

his words filtering through
stopped me in my track.

Only a Trini says-
"That beat all cockfight!"
I swung and swayed
to its rhythm.
Then I remembered-
I am a Trini woman
In a foreign place,
where they don't say
Hold Strain!
Mamaguy
Ta la la
or *Tabanca.*

In my veins
the blood of my culture
flows with the Patois
in a whirlpool of ways
to speak my mind.

A turn of phrase
can pin me to a village
in the Caribbean
where the scintillating sounds of the steelpan
at night, echo from the pan yard.

I cry in the Patois when betrayed.
Oh yo yoi!
Folks say-
Friends carry you away but they doh bring you back.

What they give you to rub you eat.

At those times when I am beset with worry
I cannot see my way out
They say-
Is who in the kitchen does feel the heat.
If you play with fire you bound to get burn.
So
Crapaud smoke you pipe!

I laugh in the patois.
On Long languid days
under *de* tamarind tree
where anything goes.
Matter fix!
Without a care in the world
in *a Vi ki vi, wajang* mood,
toute bagai!

In the Patois
I give praise to the Creator.
For the old folks say-
It better to be sure than to be cocksure.
I try to live by Moses' law
to avoid *mauvaise langue.*
For God don't like ugly

The wisdom of the old Trini proverbs
is my bridge to the past that warns me
To cut meh style to suite meh cloth
to be aware that-
Do so eh like so

and to-
don't trouble trouble
unless trouble troubles me

For I fear the day of reckoning is at hand.
One day one day Congotay!

Steelpan

Hammered and tuned from discarded oil drums,
into an instrument with light scintillating sounds,
twinkle-like, mercurial
light frothy exciting.
The first set of artisans
forged an instrument
tap tapping into a tenor pan
or the low-pitched deep-toned
bass-pan.

They worked under dilapidated tool sheds,
and broken-down huts
lit by candlelight and flambeau
in depressed neighborhoods.
Poverty stricken,
long forgotten
by King and country
but gifted and determined
to forgo the stigma
of delinquency,
they stayed the course.

Today the pan is played for royalty.
The world welcomes steelpan musicians
and their instrument, to play
Classical, Jazz, Pop and R&B.
But the Calypso and Soca rhythms
take precedence above all others.

No longer is the steelpan a relic of the backyard
but a 21st century gift
to the world of instrumentation.
Long live the Steelpan!

Shango Church

Long ago in the village,
in my infancy,
the Church took shape
from discarded wood,
with a roof of galvanized sheets
which sheltered the earthen floor.

One Sunday morn
to appease my youthful fancy,
my ten-year-old neck craned
through a crack in the wall
to take a furtive look.

The black robed priest lay prostrate
on a bed of marigold buds
screened in by dancers
in starched white cotton garb
and saffron head ties.

The narrow room-
flambeau lit
with flitting shadows
of spirit-filled disciples
speaking in tongues
invoked the goddess, Oshun.

Their strident call
and rhythmic bounce of
Wole Wole Ku Bani
Me Gba Me Gba
touched an ancient chord.

Swiftly, I was transported to a forgotten space
on the Continent of the ancestors.
There, in a clearing beneath the Balboa tree
I felt the pulse of the Bata drums
vibrating through the centuries.
They warned about a troubled future
in a new land
distant and alien
where the generations to come
would forget about lineage.

Where the myth of the Hamitic curse
slightly altered,
tailored to each century
finds new ways
to safeguard the age-old fetters
no different from chattel
still not free.
Today, the plantation is modern
multi storied glass and mortar.

The Priest

In the village where I grew up
once lived a priest,
Ecumenical by persuasion
Irish by temper.

An old curmudgeon, irascible,
with an evasive manner
and an enigmatic smile.
His speech was unclear
fuzzy and uncertain.
His dispensations vague.
For all my transgressions
of envy, pride, greed, sloth
"Say 10 Hail Marys as an act of contrition."
Said he.

For missing mass last Sunday?"
"Say 10 Hail Marys."
"But it was not my fault." Said I.
"My car was stolen."
"The weather inclement."
"My baby was ill."
"Say 10 Hail Marys!"

I wondered-
What did he say to the robber
who pilfered,
or the swindler,
or the rapist
or even the murderer-
Say 10 Hail Marys?

Making Callaloo

Dasheen bush done clean,
Yes!
Okra cut up and thrown in
with ah piece ah pumpkin.
Seasonings all clean
and cut up, cut up,
chive and onions and garlic
to boot!

Must remember to throw in
a green hot pepper
whole
to give it flavor.
Salt and cooking oil too.
I like to use a little salt butter.
You know-
the yellow butter
that we used to buy by the ounce
In Mr. Ramkissoon's grocery?

Then-
Ah grate a dry coconut
and squeeze out the milk.
After that
I light meh stove.
I put all that in de iron pot
with coconut milk and a little water
to cook.
When it all soft
and mash up, mash up

Ah take meh swizzle stick and break it down
until it look like soup
smooth,
everything mix-up, mix-up.

Wait nah!
Ah forget to take out de hot pepper!
But look at meh crosses!

The Homing Instinct

A place I know
draws me back fervently
to where my navel string is buried,
and the ancestors laid to rest.
There I once took those first steps
tentatively.

I know my home
by the imprint left of my footprints in the sand.
The shape pulls me back
often from distant places
where I choose to nest
for a while.

What of this homing instinct?
This innate sense
that beckons me
whereby the pigeon harks back to its roost
and the salmon defies all odds
to return to spawn.

What of this homing instinct?
Does it ever melt like the fallen snow,
or dissipate like an echo in the night?
Does it fade like the stars at dawn
or dries up like the dewdrops
on a blade of grass at sun up?

Maybe it is like the ebb and flow of the tide
never ceasing.

Or the mystery of the setting sun
that rises again, without fail.

It lures me home.

The Chive Planters of Paramin

From where I stood in the valley
there were flecks of color in the distance
darting to-and-fro
on the slope of the mountain.

The red-yellow-blue specks
slowly took the shape of the chive planters.
I could barely make out their form
but my gaze was drawn to the colors.

I wondered about their firm footing
to anchor themselves along the rocky slope.
How they kept their balance
tilling and tending to the chive orchards.

The hands that cared for the Allium are ancient.
They carry the intelligence of the ancestors
to sense the demands of the sunbaked
semi-arid loom of the Paramin slope.

Hands that register
the stress of drought which pull on the sap
to satisfy the thirsty land.

Sensitive touch feels for clumps-
tightened with the spread of the cluster
that with thinning, restores vigor
to the tubular leaves.

The chive planter
knows a spindly plant

without vim
can rob the essence of the bulb.

The people of the Valley
bestow custody of the chive grove
to only a few.
Their guardianship is generational,
for the chive is the most highly prized
for its flavor in Trinidad.

5
The Historic Landscape

Ole Time Days

Aye Yai Yai!
Yuh talk about ole time days?
In them days Boo-Boo man could come and get yuh–
if you back-talk to an elder or act the fool.
Then a good *cut ass*
would straighten yuh out.

On weekends we children
play marble pitch
or fashion a *Chickee-Chong* from kite paper
with a long *Zwill*-tail
fortified with razor-blades
to destroy de opponent's kite.

Box cart race, *de* game of choice,
was in vogue then,
Spinning Top and Slap Hand
a second choice.

Play was for after chores–
sweeping *de* yard with a Cocoyea broom,
or, come *foreday* morning
totin' water from *de* nearby stand pipe.
By 8 o'clock, every pipe,
bone-dry like the Sahara.
So, we had to get up real early.

I like wearing a *Sapat*,
with its noisy slip slap, slip slap

when I walk, especially after a downpour.
De sole was wooden with a foot-band
from a piece of old car tire.
(modern-day version is the slide-sandal by Nike)
without the clattering.
I remember too, my first day at school
and my first pair of *Wachekongs,*
how every night I used Blanco to
keep them clean and white.
Strange!
Present-day Sneakers remind me of them.

Every house had a tub and *Jukkin'* board
where women did all the washin'.
My mother never use bleach to whiten clothes
or soap powder.
That was still to come in *de* future.
She used imported blue soap.
She would spread her whites on a pile of stones
strategically placed
so that the midday sun could beat down on them directly.

Talking about health care.
When *yuh* feel a cold comin' on
or an upset stomach-
bush medicine was all we could afford.
It was generally prescribed by the bush doctor.
A good Sweet-Broom bath
followed by some bush tea
made from lemon grass and orange peel

which hung in bunches
 to dry in the kitchen,
for such an occasion.

For intestinal worms
every child was purged
with Castor Oil or Worm-grass tea,
a ritual done at *de* end of *de* school vacation.
Young ladies drank a tea made from
dry Bacanoe leaves for menstrual pains.

Those were *de* days without refrigeration-
when we look forward to a plate of Ma ca fourchette-
the leftovers from *de* day before.
No pot was sweeter!

Ma was a champion of
rake and scrape.
She eked out a living from bare bones,
in them hard-ass days of *Couverte Pochum*,
Coalpot, Choolha, Cockset, and flambeau,
when every man Jack was catching *de nen-nen*,
scruntin' from sunup to sundown.
Days under the lash of the Crown
with a slim chance for an education
or any decent job.
Those were hard-up, down and out times
when we ate the bread
the devil baked.

The calypsonians sing
about the virtues of Ole Time Days

The Historic Landscape

and the longing to return.
But calypsos are charged with irony and nostalgia-
sentiments you keep hidden in a box
to be examined once in a while
and replace the lid.

Past Connections

When I visit the land of my birth
I seldom see anyone I recognize
from the past.

I scan faces for a spark, a twinkle
a glimmer of recognition
a telltale sign that plays a chord
of familiarity
or a flash that says-
"Where do I know you from?"

I listen to the sounds of voices
for vocal effects-
breathy-gruff- flat- horse-low pitched-
high pitched,
evoking from past memory
an image of someone
who may have crossed my path.

I pay no heed to appearances
knowing full well Mother Time
turns a blind eye on attempts
to cheat her at her game.

Once in a while I triumph.
A voice from yesteryear hails out.
Then I can stroll down memory lane
to strengthen my hold on the place
where my ancestors are buried.

Arrival Day in Trinidad 1845
(For Dr. Ramabai Espinet)

Fatal Razack's teak bow plied the waters
on its transatlantic course
from Calcutta to Port of Spain
carrying a cargo
weighed down by the gloom of parting.

My people of Indo race and face
ancestors from elsewhere-
No-Wayrians
were shipped from pillar to post
and scattered like seeds in the sand
to germinate and reinvent themselves.

As the ship cleared the port
headed to an Indo Middle Passage
of no return, into caste and culture
according to the strictures of Kala Pani,
they became the pioneers of the migrant flow
towards the Caribbean.

Goaded along by *Backra Johnny*
from ship to shore
to barracks and fields,
a cargo of drifting forms
men and widows among them
bound coolies
setting down on the water's edge of Trinidad,
they named it Chinidad (Trinidad)
Land of Sugar.

Daily they grounded away a five-year toil
of indenture
wrestling with tropical heat and rain
feeding the hungry jaws of the mills,
for a pittance of 12 cents a day
without any rights or liberty
to come and go as they please.

Their labor fueled industry
in the Metropole
contributed to the charms of Europe
while they lived in squalor.
The irony-
creating wealth while living in poverty.

Massa day was not done yet!

Trailblazer

John Jacob Thomas,
intellectual-educator-linguist-writer
rose out of the ashes of slavery in Trinidad
like the phoenix
in the 1840's.

He was one of the lucky
to be schooled.
But many such as he
whose brilliance glowed,
were dismissed
with thumbs down
denied a fair shake,
an even break
due to their ebony hue.

Their race, for generations
had yielded forth
a sapient world of enlightenment,
in Egypt in the East
in Benin in the West
that drew Napoleon
and Alexander the Great
and all who sought insight and refinement.

A trailblazer to strike back at the Empire
his book-*Froudacity*
refuted the claims of James Anthony Froude
an acclaimed British historian
from the upper crust

who professed to know the nature of island people
from his lofty perch.

The clamor for home rule by the natives
struck a discordant chord at the Center.
Froude hastily boarded a ship down to the Caribbean
on a short fact-finding visit
to poke his nose into every open door
or to eavesdrop at every corner
seeking evidence of native ineptitude to rule themselves.
Island life was anything but idyllic
having lived under the vampiric sway for years
of the colonial coelenterate
that sucked the spoils of their labor,
and siphoned it to the Metropole.

Froude and his ilk feared governance
by the people for the people.
"They were Black
with a dark essence
that lend itself to laziness." He wrote.
"Not fit to govern!"

Thomas in a succinct rebuttal
ripped apart those claims
citing hastiness and bigotry.
His book - *Froudacity*
chronicled the audacity of Froude
to make hasty judgements
of an entire group of people
just from a cursory glance.

Such was the beginning of
a slow movement of protest
taken up later by C.L.R James
and Eric Williams, James Padmore and others
who embarked on a journey in the twentieth century
for Independence.
They worked towards the day
when they could say to the likes of Froude.

"The slings and arrows of outrageous fortune…"
We can bear on our own!

Indigenous

They were here when Columbus came.
Lokono Arawaks and Caribs
in the Land of the Humming Bird
which they named Iere
in their native tongue.
Columbus in a first act of erasure
renamed it *La Isla de la Trinidad,*
the island of the Trinity.

None of them survived the onslaught.
Do we say that they are as 'Dead as a Dodo?'
Do we say they are extinct?
Animals are extinct, birds and T-Rex.
Are people?
To be extinct is to be obliterated.
Irrecoverable,
without trace or culture.

The Extinction Vortex and the Orbis Spike
provide several models for human extirpation
but none closely relates to the European assault
and its effect on first nations-
peoples, ravished by epidemics
their blood watered down
by miscegenation.

For centuries the virgin land
echoed the call of the cacique
mingled with the grating toucan sounds

and the shrieking parrots.
In some wonderful mystical way
remnants of their ways
survive in the collective unconscious of people
who carry traces of their bloodline.

Their staple foods-
Cassava and sweet potatoes,
we still oil-down
with coconut cream,
breadfruit and callaloo bush
in the tangy, citrusy
flavors of old.

The 'wild meat' they hunted
the Agouti, Lapp and Tattoo
was roasted and cooked over an open fire,
done in Lokono fashion
to seal in the juices.
My mother, on special occasions
curried it in the traditional cast-iron pot,
over a hot stove.

Food is the link
that lures us to the Lokono past here in Trinidad.
Their language swallowed and consumed
was once written in rock-art engravings.

When the Lokono people
shared their communal fare,
their music must have been sung
in the pentatonic scale

to accompany the tapotement sounds
of the slap, slapping percussion
of wrist on body.
The Swedes have adopted the technique
into a type of massage stroke today.

This tendency for Old World contact
with the New, in a collision of worlds
led to enslavement,
spread of diseases, exploitation,
decline of community and culture
suppression of religion,
language, and a loss of tribal lands.

Did it balance out with the exchanges of knowledge
technology and agricultural practices
not suited to the new climes?
Their insights of the natural world
for the good of the community
went unheeded by the visitors
blinded by the mesmerizing shine
of yellow gold.

The Columbian Exchange of plants-
of cash crops of sugar cane, wheat and tobacco
had its own reverberating sounds
down the centuries
which started with Columbus.

Today, native peoples in places he once set foot
are cursed with devastation
population displacement

and environmental destruction
all in the interest of wealth
and exploitation.

Such is the price of modernity and change.

The Merikins of Moruga

The Merikins were African-American slaves who supported the British in the war of 1812 in America. When the British lost, they settled some of them in the colonies of the British Empire, in Canada, Jamaica, the Bahamas and in Trinidad, in the village of Moruga. They called themselves, Merikins, a patois word derived from the word, Americans. There are still descendants of this group living in Trinidad today.

> When I visited
> the aged griot in Moruga,
> a descendant of the Merikins, he said-
> "It was dem to catch!"
>
> That set me thinking
> about the fetters of chattel slavery
> and runaway slaves.
> I imagine
> their whole existence
> must center on freedom.
>
> "Some ah dem slave masters in America
> was bad like crab!" He continued.
> "Black folks catch de nen nen on
> some ah them plantation. But there is an old
> African saying- 'One day one day Congotay!'"
>
> In my poet's eye I piece together a scene of desolation.
> I reckon all that was allowed to them
> were the many leaps of imagination
> and their dreams.
> Dreams were important.

Without dreams, there can be no striving
towards the implausible.

"Oh, de masters had de power, all right
but some of them slaves had de craft.
Freedom was in their blood." He said.
I imagine the mythological character Sisyphus,
like the slave master,
he is set on pushing that rock,
his bondsman, uphill
to the highest point-
the breaking point.

The moment Sisyphus slackens his grip
the rock rolls back down the hill
and escapes his grasp,
severing his hold.
Sisyphus tries again and again
always pushing, always demanding
with the same result.

"Santimanitay, without mercy!"
The old man whispered.
There have been many such bond-releasing forces
throughout chattel history
when the master was not looking.

"When push come to shove, some ah them
run away and join the army."
The old man's words interrupted my thoughts.
Sometimes war was the answer.
Such was the war of 1812, for instance-

the enslaved on American soil
considered:
that the enemy of my enemy
was my friend.
So, they joined the British forces
as did the Black loyalists
during the American Revolution
half a century before.
It was a pack-
combat in exchange for freedom.

The 1812 war-
often referred to
as the forgotten war
was a mishmash of colors and culture
Indigenous peoples, runaway slaves
British, American, some French.
Each fighting for his own personal gain.

The enslaved were aligned with
their ancient captor- the British,
who were bent on teaching a lesson on warfare
to the truant break-away colony of America.

When the dust settled
victory was awarded to the young nation.
The British, crushed by defeat,
pulled up roots expeditiously
to make a hasty retreat.
They took with them
their former runaway slaves
who had fought with them in combat.

Some they settled in Nova Scotia
some back to Africa in Sierra Leone
and over 500 in Trinidad,
a waystation in the Caribbean-
a colonial backdrop.

Sir Ralph Woodford,
the British governor in Trinidad,
at the time,
provided sanctuary
awarding a plot of 16 acres of Virgin territory
to each freedman
to clear and shape
into his own idea of freedom.

"When they put foot in Moruga
they shouted 'Massa day done!'" He cried.
"They had to rake and scrape
for years before they could make a penny off the land.
But it was freedom!"

The land!
that was not the ancestral land.
But by hook or by crook
they found a home in Moruga
to create a watershed moment
in the history of Trinidad.
"Dem was real pioneers
the early Merikins of Moruga." He quipped
with pride in his voice.

And I thought
that unlike life on the plantation
they were able to forge a legacy
out of virgin territory
for their children.
Some of the descendants
their great great grandchildren still
make their home in Moruga.
Even to this day!

Idlewild, Michigan
(Dedicated to Joe Les and Eric J. Lindsey
and their cousin Ernestine Reed)

A crooked shoreline hems in Lake Idlewild's
tranquil fresh-standing water-wonder
with no fixed determination
to go anywhere,
not to empty into a river or the sea.
Still, at intervals a moving current
with a calm ripple crops up,
as the wind skips over her surface.

On the coastal zone,
a school of guppies swim-
fan tailing along the water's edge in pairs-
the male, small and colorful
just a tad distance behind her
flicking his caudal and dorsal fins
to attract her attention.

I reach down to dip my hand into the warm water
in a ritual of returning to the cradle-
to Idlewild, the town, the aging mother
who has lived through the seasons of her life.
I feel a wistful affection for her past.

Her Spring, once marked the unfolding
the birth of an idea
a place that could be a haven
to raise and nurture her people.

The legacy years of summer's blooms-
flamboyant regalia, rich and trendy
Rhythm and Blues, Jazz
the Swing and Cha Cha Cha
Twisting the night away
with the Jitterbug
were happy times, safe in the sanctuary
of her bosom.

Then the Autumn years and the 60's
for her brood, a time of spring-
jejune and curious.
One by one they left the nest
to sample new fruits,
once forbidden
now hanging low but perilous of reach.

She is now in her winter years
when loneliness and the fading is fast.
She struggles to scale an upward ascent
amidst all hope.
For her, the seasons will never be a cycle.

Occasionally. she is visited by the young
who are set on keeping her alive
for she was once the Eden, the open door
where Black people
hastened to enter.

Mackinaw Island

The Ojibwe, Odawa and Potawatomi peoples
of Mackinaw traded felt and fur with the white man
for wampum,
rifles, pots and pans, knives and copper.
After 300 years of trade
they had to destroy their beaver traps.

Where once they trapped only as needed,
with European contact and the demand for fur
their relation with the beaver, the mink, lynx
entered into a system of commerce.
No longer did they hear the warnings of the ancestors.

Then the fashion in Europe changed-
Beaver hats went out of vogue,
but by then the beaver dams lay silent
crumbling apart-piece by piece-from over-hunting.
It took 150 years for the beaver to recover,
slowly emerging after
the halt on entrapment.

Thinking of the ancestors of Mackinaw
I climbed 208 steps to Arch Rock
a circular portal in the rock
where it is said the spirits of the ancestors
passed through to paradise.

On Mackinaw Island their chiefs were buried
for centuries, on earthen mounds
such as on the rise where the Grand Hotel sits

overlooking Lake Huron.
Some bones have been returned to the tribes.

Mackinaw is a haven for tourist-
the scent of chocolate and fudge
seep onto the main streets
drawing them in for a taste.

It is a horse's haven, their hooves
clippety-clopping their way
with a sound that takes you back in time.
A man walks around with a shovel and bucket,
when without any regard for propriety
the horses, with a hearty fart of disdain
relieve themselves anywhere on the trail-
to the Grand or along the route to the sights.
He scoops up the dung
as cyclists duck and weave to avoid
sliding in a pool of piss.

Four-wheeled vehicles are banned
to ensure the freshness of the air for the horses.
With a whiff mingling with the scent of fudge
you can smell the horsey loamy musky
barn-yard vinegary animalic scent of horse
up and down the trails.

The floral gardens stopped my pace.
I reveled in the display of flowers-
from the large and showy Rudbeckias
towering over the subtle Sedum

to splashes of colorful Petunias
like in a Monet-type portrayal of his
Le Jardin de Monet a Giverny

I am charmed
by flowers nodding downwards
to passersby
or reaching to the sky
to pay tribute.
The hollow-stem Dahlia
tall in a carnivalesque display
bearing her queenly blossoms
is surrounded by a kaleidoscope of colorful annuals
signaling to the pollinators-
birds, butterflies, bees.
I rejoiced in this floral tapestry!

Fron the cardinal points
you can see the steeple of the old St Anne's Church
the stained glass beckoned me.
On a wall is a painting
of an Algonquin-Mohawk woman-
a Roman Catholic saint
known as Kateri Tekakwitha
who died in 1680 and canonized in 2012.

All along the bike trail
are markers of the early native inhabitants.
A small museum on Market Street
chronicles their struggles
to keep their ancestral lands.

Visitors to Mackinaw drift in and out casually
on their way to the fort which overlooks the museum.
As they leave, an Odawa woman on a recording
announces that her people are still here on Mackinaw!

History

To Susan A Delaney, a History buff

What of our nation's recorded history?
Should it be laid to rest in catacombs
and sealed sarcophagus
never to be opened and examined?

Should we say that it is in the past
and exempt from further scrutiny.
That recorded history is sacrosanct,
factual and sacred
immutable-fixed in time
settled, ageless, enduring?

They query-
Why disturb the clouds of dust
that long settled into a comfortable repose?
Let sleeping dogs lie!
Why wake the hound
dozing in the arms of Morpheus?

Or should we declare history as contrived
managed
the handmaiden of the Bourgeois
cleansed, classified, racialized-gendered
in which the subaltern cannot speak
the plebian has no voice
and sanitized myth triumphs
where truth fades
in silence
with each passing year?

Whose history is being told?
Is there room for the victims?
Today, the conquest of the Americas
speaks of heroism.
What of the violence, hunger, exploitation
buried in accounts of progress?
Who speaks for the Arawaks Caribs Aztecs
Incas Powhatans Pequots
the Igbo Yoruba Cherokee?
History clamors for survival
to be relevant
instructive, inclusive
of the choir of voices
anxious to be heard.

So let us re-examine the past
perchance to rectify falsities
that wore the cloak of certainty
for too long.
For History should be the gift
we all partake of–
a bequest for generations.

Not solely to uplift the few.

The Wretched of this Earth

> "Give me your tired, your poor,
> Your huddled masses yearning to breathe free,
> The wretched refuse of your teeming shore
> Send these, the homeless, tempest-tossed, to me,
> I lift my lamp beside the golden door!"
>
> -Emma Lazarus

To which I respond:

And so, they came in droves,
From countries far and wide.
With tongues Germanic and Romance,
In speech and idiom pride,

Led through the Golden door,
Into a promised land,
To rise and spread
To thrive and grow,
To breathe and to expand.

To bar entry of the colored race
The indigent and hapless poor,
those dispossessed of land and fate
Fanon's Wretched of the Earth.

Covid 19

COVID 19 creeps through the cracks of greed
spreading from creek to peak
across oceans of indifference,
inflamed by a carnal disregard
for this orb-a gift, leveraged
milked and pimped
for the mighty dollar.

COVID 19's artillery of variants
outflank the fighting force
of mortals, defenseless
against an invisible foe,
her retributive justice
baffling the rational mind
accustomed to cause and effect.

COVID 19 cautions the meddlers
tinkering with the species
pushing the barriers
to exploit the commercial value of wildlife
in over harvesting
which disturbs the food chain.

From her utmost
Nature's pecking order
unfolds from the highest
to the lowest.
The music of creation
flows from measure to measure
each note -a genus

contributing to the form
of the melody,
her sole right to orchestrate.

Hers is an awe-inspiring symphony
harmoniously conducted
but when tampered with,
alters the tempo, a delicate equilibrium
balancing beauty and brutality
to unleash a trail of tears.

Covid 19 and sisters SARS and MERS
are modern diseases.
Genera that were once apart now meld
where a virus in a Zoonotic leap
can hop a short ride
to rest for a while in an intermediate host
before it reaches its final destination-
Homo sapiens intricate network of blood vessels
where it wreaks havoc
in the spawning of another pathogen.

Such is COVID 19.

Three Fifths

The Three Fifths Compromise
untethered the restraints
on human bondage,
slowly frittering away
the moral rectitude
that anchored the enslaver
at times- uneasily,
to the "peculiar institution."

 1787 flouted the handiwork of the Creator
who shape all things complete.
But of the African,
1787 claimed incomplete
with three fifths done?

The voice of the church
in a deafening silence
capitulated to Mammon,
made no claim
for the moral issue.

Why then proselytize those traditional faiths
whose cosmology
emphasize completeness
in their relation between
God and creation?
And their willingness to dialog
with the deities
on equal terms
signifying wholeness?

The Three Fifths Compromise
curtsied to the spread
of plantation economies.
At its heart, chattel slavery
beating to the drum of the cotton gin
and the Indian Removal Act
by seizure of Indigenous lands.

The unholy marriage
of the South-King Cotton
Lords of the lash
with the North-
Lords of the loom
Looming mills
were of a dance
of cash and cargo.

The Three Fifths Compromise
paved the way for the Trail of Tears
misery
which still echoes through the veil of time.

The Weeping Time
(for Pat Betts)

>"ADVERTISEMENT
>
>*SALE*
>
>***NEGROES FOR SALE!***
>*440 men women children*
>*Available for Inspection*
>*Venue: Savannah*
>*Ten Broeck Race Course*
>*2nd – 3rd March 1859*
>*Time: 10am to 6pm."*

An account of a time of weeping:
A Jeremiad against the "peculiar institution"
a sale of chattel
to settle the debts of its owner of Butler Island-
Pierce Mease Butler.

And so, it was said
it rained for two days
to wash away the woeful tears
of mothers
as their children clung to their breasts.
Thirty children with fearful eyes
sold like lambs to the slaughter.

Young people, defying convention
who were pierced by cupid's arrow
pleaded with the buyer

to be sold together.
We know nothing of their beauty
for beauty in the Black
was in the future
when Stokely deemed it beautiful.
But mention was made
only of the value invested in hands-
a full hand or half hand or small hand
and hips-broad enough to breed.
For, worth in the time of weeping
was value laden-
products to be packaged and sold,
business as usual.
Since the Spirit of the Age counseled-
'Gain wealth forgetting all but self'.

At the Savannah auction
the Geechie people of Butler Island
wept with the downpour
of God's tears mingling
with their sorrow
and the chains that bind.
The pain of parting
weaves its gossamer strands
linking the generations
through the Middle Passage
to the plantation,
never to cease
in the time of chattel
stamped with the pain of separation.

That fateful auction-
was a stone throw in time
from the evil war of the brothers
when siblings fought each other
for the freedom to enslave others.
Pierce Mease Butler
a weak and profligate man,
gambled away his boomerang-shaped, Butler Island
floating on the Altamaha River
fenced in by brackish water.

The day-by-day toil of his slaves
shaped the virgin land
into wealth.
In the act of winnowing,
his fortune like chaff
was blown away by the winds of chance
his debt to be settled in the labor
of his bondsmen, women and children
on the auction block.

For generations the Gullah people
of Butler Island
lived off the land and the waters.
They carried the memory
of their ancestors from the African coast,
and the ways of the rice, cotton and indigo
while working on communal lands.

They gave praise in the Geechee
Anglicized in a new way

with words dressed from memory
of the past-
always in a struggle to be heard
that refused to be quiet and forgotten
remnants of the Igbo or Yoruba or Hausa.

What of this fateful time of weeping?
This time of separation
brother from brother
sister from sister
children from parents
and lovers apart?

Why talk about it?
Or erect markers to draw attention
to the evil of human bondage?
Of the nature of chattel
that can be bought sold
exchange settled for debts
mortgaged gifted
all without regard for the human?

Because-
History is cunning.
It creeps and crawls in disguise,
always seeking revival
to rebound
when least expected.

At Kent State, May 4th 1970

When the First Amendment, stripped
of its rank by the Primacy of Force
so skillfully executed as, first, to-give
the impression of retreat, a maneuver
so dazzling-as to confuse-but-then
suddenly to pivot into an attack
on students unarmed- ripe-for
the cutting, all standing
row after row-poised
for execution,
without knowing
the error of their ways
by protesting
an unjust war-
that day
Vietnam
had come
to America
At Kent.

Roe v Wade
(June 24, 2022)

Today we are powerless to
hold onto what little control
the right to privacy
implicit in the 14th Amendment
once bestowed.

We are told there is no longer
a constitutional right
to free choice.
After the 1973 ruling, we celebrated
a period of pro-choice that slowly took
a fifty-year downhill slide
finally, to be told-
there is to be no exception
for rape or incest.

Choice has lost out
to be solely in the hands of a few.
The nativist-evangelicals have won out
fearing their numerical decline,
but it will also unleash a surge in numbers
among POC.

Monticello

The tour bus slowly inches up the ascent
along the hilly slope
hugging the spiral asphalt strip
leading to the top of the hill.

Patient as a sentinel
the Jefferson nickel-view
captures Monticello's gaze
across the Blue Ridge Mountains.

On the northern side, my poet's eye
sees through the haze of history
forms- Black   Brown   Light,
balancing bright buckets in a single file
coursing up a steep path
from the shallow stream below
up to the mansion house-
a tabernacle erected for the Founder.

My matter-of-fact ways
which can border on the humdrum-
dull, mundane aspect of life
ponder over this house on the hill
so far away from the elixir of life.

My island nature
taps into the undercurrent of despair
that once hemmed in the captive,
like an armor plate.
The shadow of the yoke still hangs over this place

for it knows the tether between past and present
is unbroken.

I sense the repulse of unfamiliar hands
probing inner sanctums
of chattel women,
whose fierce silence
faced the blade of bondage
in a denial of their agency.
Always with uncertainty
the walls of their world were not built for progeny.
At any moment cracks in the rampart could give way
to release a torrent
sweeping away the bonds
tied to children, mothers, fathers
enroute to the slave block.

 I travel to the hilltop
in search of the Founding Father
who for a quarter century
is sometimes masked in the raiment
of a saint
other times of the unholy.

I step through the doorway
into the entrance hall of Monticello
a shrine to the naturalist
of antlers- moose, elk and deer,
Native American hunting gear
rain-dance sticks, African vintage spear
and a pair of woman's moccasins.

I wander into the study
to force my myopic eye to read the titles
of ancient tomes stacked high up to the ceiling.
I perceive an interest in Astronomy
Cartography, printing, music and time.

I climb the winding staircase
to the upper rooms
clothed in restraint and austerity
with no touch of the whimsical
no frills or flowery décor,
no handprints of the feminine
and I wonder about
the two mothers, half-sisters.

Sandy Hook and Others

Experts say-
School shootings are more likely to occur
in small rural towns,
with low crime rates
where everyone knows your name
where it's safe to bring up children.

A long-time resident says-
"This is not supposed to happen here!"
Where is here?
The Sandy Hooks of USA?
Places where few of us have ever entered
the main street.
Or if perchance we did
through expedience
the stare is so cold you could chisel the words-
"Not Welcome!"

The perpetrator is no stranger,
he may have crossed their threshold
or sat at the local diner across from them
or worshiped at the local Bible Church,
or rode the bus with their children.
They know his tendencies,
his disposition, his proclivity like a bent rod
ever drawn inwards towards
a river of turmoil that
quenches his thirst for violence.

They saw his postings.
Heard his rants
but small towners don't interfere
don't dip into other people's business.
Besides it's just a phase
he'll outgrow it.

Afterall
"Mass murder is not supposed to happen here!"

Sundown Town
(To Kaaba Brunson)

It was not listed in the Green Book.
In those days
how did a parent or a teacher or a religious leader,
the mayor or the man in the street
respond to a child's question-
"Tell me why we call our town Anna?"
There used to be a tell-tale sign
on Highway 127, in the 1970s.

Once there were as many as ten thousand towns
"From sea to shining sea."
From Alix, Arkansas,
To Zephyrhills, Florida
To Edmond, Oklahoma-
"A good place to live… no Negroes."
Cumberland, Tennessee, in 1900 touted-
"No Malaria, No Mosquitoes and No Negroes."
Comanche County trumpeted-
we are "the purest Anglo-Saxon population
in the United States."

Sundowned into mediocrity
The Lash Law in Eugene was the harbinger of woe
for those who tarried after nightfall.

The pariah -
once held to be three fifths
conferred status on those
who wrestled with history.

To resist peeling the privilege off whiteness
at nightfall,
sundowners were deputized
to torture, violate or murder at will.

Migrants to find havens in the north
discovered ways to identify places to avoid-
towns with names-
Palm-this or White-that.

Popular culture invented the Black.
A shuffling, wide-grinning,
happy-go-lucky
dancing, loud-laughing minstrelsy caricature.
A code of exclusion to keep him at bay.

 Ubiquitous Minstrel shows
fixed the image of the Back tropes
which later became the handmaiden of Eugenics.

Then there was the *Birth of a Nation*
first screened in the White House.
In attendance was Woodrow Wilson
and his cabinet.
The occasion-
a fitting dress rehearsal for the Klan's
extrajudicial violence.

Sundowners' absurd
"If You Can Read …You'd Better Run…
If You Can't Read …You'd Better Run Anyway"
co-opted the role of Sisyphus

to the outsider
in a futile up the hill
down again rolling rock.

In Slocum, Texas
in Mt. Olive and Gillespie and Pana, Illinois
in the 1960s
Black motorist could not buy gas.
Stranded in these towns
they were warned-
"Don't let the sun set on you here, understand?"

Came the 1960s, the cleansing freeze
slowly melted.
The warning signs from the roadside
came down.
Outsiders filtered in to settle
across the tracks
or on the fringes of town
separated by Martin Luther King Drive.

To circumvent blending with the castaways
the suburban drift-
gated into seclusion
was led by a new impulse
to be sealed off into exurbs
behind walls of lofty oaks and elms.

Twenty first century
curated selection of "enclavers"
are now the heirs apparent to the sundowners
of yesteryear.

Safeguarded through ordinances
homeowners' associations
and astute brokers
the sentinels of exclusivity
sound a new Clarion call for marketability.
Ensconced behind a barrier reef of protection
Gentrification and redlining
the racial sprawl is halted
as effectively as a Sundown town warning.

www.ingramcontent.com/pod-product-compliance
Lightning Source LLC
Chambersburg PA
CBHW022238201224
19322CB00017BA/595